# The American Utopian Adventure

*SERIES TWO*

## THE HUTTERITES

# The Hutterites; A Study in Social Cohesion

BY

LEE EMERSON DEETS

ASSOCIATE PROFESSOR OF SOCIOLOGY
UNIVERSITY OF SOUTH DAKOTA

WITH A NEW EPILOG BY THE AUTHOR

AND AN APPENDIX

*The Origins of Conflict in the
Hutterische Communities*

## PORCUPINE PRESS

*Philadelphia 1975*

First edition 1939
(Gettysburg: privately printed, 1939)


Reprinted with additions 1975 by
PORCUPINE PRESS, INC.
Philadelphia, Pennsylvania 19107

**Library of Congress Cataloging in Publication Data**

Deets, Lee Emerson, 1898-
  The Hutterites.

  (The American utopian adventure, series two)
  Reprint of the ed. published at Gettysburg, Pa.,
which was issued as the author's thesis, Columbia, 1939.
  Includes bibliographical references.
  1.  Hutterite Brethren.  I.  Title.
BX8129.H8D4   1975      289.7'3        74-26737
ISBN 0-87991-029-1

*Manufactured in the United States of America*

To the memory of

R. K. D.

# TABLE OF CONTENTS

# PREFACE

On a bluff on the South Dakota side of the broad valley of the Missouri River where it winds between South Dakota and Nebraska, lies a secluded, peaceful little village of religious communists whose buildings, dress, customs, and whole way of living and thinking contrast strikingly with the world around them. The community, known as Old Bon Homme, is one of forty-nine Hutterite communities in the United States and Canada. Old Bon Homme and her seventeen daughter colonies constitute the field of investigation in this study.

From almost the first moment of entrance into the Bon Homme colony of Hutterites in the autumn of 1929, I was curious to know how the order operated. Were one able to take it apart, what operation and gearing of parts would account for its functioning? What combination of factors operates to make the continuance of such a variant and unique manner of living possible, surrounded as it is by twentieth century America? Inquiry revealed an amazingly long history of over four centuries, more than two centuries longer than any other of the communities of its kind, commonly called Utopian. The problem of how the order operates was evidently a problem as to how it had long continued to operate, a problem in social cohesion. The social cohesion of a communal, religious order became the problem of this investigation. How have the Hutterites cohered?

Answer to the question was to become the goal of a quest through the spare time of subsequent years. The question was taken into most of the Hutterite colonies in South Dakota, Manitoba and Alberta. It was carried into the sharing of their common life and work in field, mill, work-shop, and home. It was the subject of discussion in eager groups packed into Hutterite homes, later to be pondered at night beneath high-piled feather ticks. It was in the background in the sharing of their joys and sorrows— the gay celebration of the wedding feast and the hush and sad wonder at the death bed. The question led to scrutiny of records of vital statistics, of Hutterite archives and business records in German long-hand script, and of newspaper accounts of the Hutterites during the time they have been in Dakota Territory and South Dakota. Threads were sought in their long and stirring history. Diaries and intimate correspondence were made available. Interviews to construct personal case histories were given. Ex-Hutterites, neighbors, business associates, and officials who had contact with the Hutterites in South Dakota and Manitoba were interviewed. The inquiry was carried afield to comparable communities and formerly existing communities of their kind, in visits to Amana, the Shakers, Zoar, the Doukhobors, the House of David, Oneida and many others. The result might be called a case study of the cohesion of a social order.

Much of the material cannot be included in this present study which has the character of a summary of points relevant to cohesion. Perhaps most significant of the material omitted in part has been that which relates to recent threats to their cohesion due to the penetration of influences from outside. It seems more fitting too to publish with a larger work the bibliography which relates to it. As a remedy for this shortcoming, within the ensuing year a much larger work, now partly finished, entitled, "The Hutterites; Communal City of God," will be offered for publication.

Specific acknowledgment of indebtedness to the host of those who have given aid, would require many pages. It is a matter of much regret that they cannot be acknowledged personally. The list would include many Hutterites and Hutterite communities. To the members of the Department of Sociology of Columbia University I am much indebted, for instruction, guidance, inspiration and encouragement, and especially to Professor R. M. MacIver who has been director of the study from the beginning, and to Professor R. S. Lynd who has also given much of his time to offer valuable suggestions and encouragement. I am also indebted to Professor Gardner C. Murphy before one of whose classes much of this work was presented at length for criticism, and to Dr. Erich Fromm whose psychoanalytic insights made the Hutterite personality more intelligible.

Of those of my Hutterite friends who may feel that certain discordant notes in their community life should not have been sounded, I beg them to see my problem of loyalty to truth even as one of their historians and bishops, Johannes Waldner, saw his, when he wrote, "I would much rather pass over this in silence, and suffered much at the thought of having to hand down to our descendants the memory of our shortcomings, but I was compelled against my will to write the same, first because I did not dare to omit part and thus not write the truth in my history, . . . second because our experiences can be a warning to us and to our descendants."[1]

---

[1] *From* a translation by Johann Loserth in "The Decline and Revival of the Hutterites," *Mennonite Quarterly Review,* Vol. IV, April 1930, p. 106.

# CHAPTER I

## The Collective Security of a Cohesive Order

The communal religious sect known as Hutterites presents an unusual opportunity for study of group cohesion. The sect has existed for more than four centuries. It is the patriarch of the Utopian communities, the first and oldest of the several hundred idealistic community groups in Europe and America which have attempted to create more perfect social orders. The Hutterite order has outlived all other Utopian communities by two and one-half centuries. The group still thrives, five thousand strong, in forty-nine communities scattered over the prairies of South Dakota, Manitoba, and Alberta. There is no present basis for saying that the end is in sight.

The Hutterite order may be described as a microcosmic one, existing within and paralleling our own. The Hutterites have kept their order in the face of changes which have remade our own western world. When the communal Hutterite order was established, modern commercial capitalism was coming into being and the modern nation state was emerging. The resurgence of science in the eighteenth century which was to transform the western world into a technological civilization was yet to appear. The capacity of the Hutterites to resist change has been a phenomenal characteristic.

Most of the Hutterite communities exhibit a degree of peacefulness, social harmony, and cohesion which by contrast with our society is very striking. Within their order they have collective security. Without aid of relief, public or private, Hutterites in South Dakota have remained solvent taxpayers in a state in which one-third of the population has been on relief, in which seventy-five per cent of the banks have failed, and in which taxes have become delinquent on approximately one-third of the taxable land.[1]

---

[1] W. F. Kumlein, *A Graphic Survey of the Relief Situation in South Dakota,* Agricultural Experiment Station Bulletin 310, May 1937, Brookings, S. D., pp. 11-20.

Crime, either against our society or their own, is very rare. Divorce is unknown. Almost all members of Hutterite society have extraordinary mental health and freedom from mental conflicts and tensions. Family quarrelling does not exist. They assert that quarrelling of any kind is extremely rare. Suicide has never occurred. Insanity is almost non-existent. The prolonged neurotic anxiety which may be found in our society is almost nonexistent. The society is very nearly classless. The Hutterites are not disturbed by struggle for success or recoil which comes with sense of failure. Economically speaking, neither success nor failure are part of their pattern of living. Lonesomeness and friendlessness are practically unknown. Even death is quite universally viewed with an equanimity born of assurance that it is but a transition into an eternal future life. Few Hutterites have intellectual problems which are a source of mental conflict. Truths are held as absolutes and a sufficient number have been established as such to provide satisfying answers to individual problems. As compared with our society, the Hutterite community is an island of certainty and security in a river of change.

In our world outside the Hutterite colonies the present is a time when people are giving thought anew to problems of cohesive order. Security is being thought of as collective. Many have sacrificed freedom for collective order while probably many more are apprehensive lest they must. Neither the Hutterites nor the writer regard their order as a world panacea. The salient fact is that in a world desperately searching for order, the Hutterites have it in full measure. However one may feel about the desirability of the Hutterite order, the fact of its cohesiveness and its demonstrated persistence through four centuries remains. Their long experiment stands as a challenge to our capacity to understand how a group can so long cohere. It is to the problem of cohesion that this study is directed. History, description, and other problems identified with the Hutterite community will be introduced only insofar as they have a bearing upon the central problem of cohesion.

# CHAPTER II

## The Time Setting

The first Hutterite community, though not yet bearing the name, was established southeast of Brunn (now Brno) in Moravia in 1528.[1] The founders were German-speaking refugees, known as Anabaptists, who were fleeing from persecution during the time of the Protestant Reformation.

Like many other Utopian communities the Hutterite community came out of a background of protest and a desire to escape to a more satisfying form of order. At the time of Hutterite origins central Europe was in a revolutionary state of disorder. Great masses of the population had been unmoored from their anchoring in the Roman Catholic church. Harassing economic conditions had culminated in a bloody peasants' war. Leaders of church and state united in suppressing what they regarded as a dangerous threat to established institutions. Deserted by Reformation leaders, great numbers of peasants and towns-people turned elsewhere for order. They were inspired by Humanistic influences to search anew the original Christian sources. This they did by turning to the German translation of the New Testament which had been made by Martin Luther in 1524. The result was a highly ethical, community-centered system of beliefs, emphasizing communal philanthrophy and pacifism, based upon a literal interpretation of brotherhood as a family relationship extended to the community. Persecutors were looked upon as evil. Persecutors and their ways, in fact, their world, were to be avoided, as of the devil. Such was the Reformation and Anabaptist background of Hutterite origins.

---

[1] Primary sources for Hutterite historic references used in this chapter are their own chronicles, the *Grosse Geschicht-Buch* and the *Kleine Geschicht-Buch*. The former has been edited and published; *Geschicht-Buch der Hutterischen Brueder,* Rudolph Wolkan (editor), Wien, 1923.

3

The Hutterites differentiated themselves from other Anabaptists by their emphasis upon communality. During the eight-year period, 1528 to 1536, their system emerged from loose organization around philanthropic communality to organization around complete consumers' and producers' communism. Communism, pacifism, and avoidance of the world, are today the three central Hutterite doctrines of living. All are held as Biblically based.

Influential factors in the emergence and early survival of the Hutterite order were homogeneity of membership, persecution, the adoption of producers' communism, and strong leadership. Homogeneity developed through a process of elimination. Dissenters left. As a result of very severe persecution members of the struggling community felt a keen sense of oneness as fellow-sufferers from a common enemy. Producers' communism was established by a strong leader. Strong leadership, more than anything else, accounts for the successful emergence of a unified, autonomous, Hutterite ideology.

Members of the early Hutterite experiment got their first stabilizing coherence by grouping themselves around a dominant, confidence-inspiring personality. Jacob Huter, from whom the Hutterites derive their name, may be credited with the triple contribution of drawing the Hutterites together around himself, giving them a working ideology, and directing the development of the institutional organization for living in accordance with the ideology. He was assisted by another strong leader, Peter Riedemann, when the latter was not in prison. When Huter became leader of the group in 1533 it was held together by little else than the external pressure of persecution. Within the year he persuaded his followers that to prevent discord and achieve ideal brotherhood they must adopt full communism. Some of the cohesive loyalty which they gave to him he was able to transfer to his communal ideology. It is significant for Hutterite survival that Huter, unlike many subsequent Utopian community leaders, did not leave the group organized around the precarious stability of a personality. It is also significant that within three years he was able to fashion an institutional system which worked. His work was accomplished none too soon, for in 1536 he was burned at the stake at Innsbruck.

Members during the early history of a Utopian community usually face two critical tests, first, necessity to transfer loyalties from a dominant personality to an ideology as a cohesive focus, and second, to adjust, themselves to the new way of living for which the ideology provides. Huter led his people through the first difficult period, and Riedemann, who assumed control in 1542, led them through the second. He held the group together until the system became institutionalized, capable of self-perpetuation chiefly by means of indoctrination and habituation. After Riedemann, institutional authority replaced leadership. Men who aspired to personal leadership were distrusted as threatening the traditions.

### THE CHRONICLES

However, it is doubtful whether the Hutterites could have so long adhered to the traditions had they not had a written source of authority regarding them. Chief Hutterite sources are two volumes of their history written by their own recorders year by year as events occurred and as new issues were clarified. The books might be described as community diaries. They are the *Grosse Geschicht-Buch* or Great Chronicle and the *Kleine Geschicht-Buch* or Little Chronicle. In the Great Chronicle, by far the most important of the two, the first 137 years of Hutterite history is recorded. During the first part of this period the Hutterites reached a probable maximum of 25,000, and achieved what they regard as their most ideal stage of development.[2] They refer to it as "the ideal time of the Church." The historic record of the ideal period is constantly used as a source for definition of doctrine and procedure. The Great Chronicle serves both as a common law code, though written, and as a handbook for guidance in following the code and enforcing its sanctions.

The Great Chronicle is also an extraordinary record of martyrdom. While it was being written more than two thousand members were put to death, many by devious methods of torture.

---

[2] This estimate was given to the writer orally by Eberhart Arnold, Ph.D., a native of Germany and organizer of the German Youth Movement who recently organized the contemporary European Hutterite colonies and whom the writer regarded as the most outstanding authority upon the Hutterites.

Hundreds were taken into Turkey as slaves. Dozens of colonies were destroyed. The "ideal period" was followed by slaughter, enslavement, rape, arson and plundering. The Great Chronicle's pages depicting martyrdom are powerful reagents upon Hutterite emotions. When the Hutterite reads them or tells of them, the deep flow of emotion which show his true character is revealed. He becomes one with the ideal *"Hutterische"* way, the "only true and right way." He loses himself in oneness with an order which has had a long, historic continuity through time. It is to the many pages about the martyrs that the Hutterite turns in times of crisis when in need of strength, solace and courage. He too must be willing to die for *Die Glauben,* the beliefs. The Great Chronicle is more than a code and a handbook. It has within its pages a powerfully energizing source for inspiring loyalty to the codes. The Little Chronicle, which brings Hutterite history up to 1824, also tells of hardships, particularly during migration. It is primarily a record of migration.

During approximately the first three and one-half centuries the Hutterites kept migrating eastward toward new frontiers, from Moravia to Hungary and Transylvania, to Wallachia and finally to Ukraine. The cyclical movement was a saving factor in their survival. As each frontier became settled and population closed in around them they moved on to newer isolation. During the years 1874 to 1879 three colonies of them, comprising a total of about 250 persons, migrated to Dakota Territory in America to settle in what is now southeastern South Dakota. This frontier too became settled and in 1918 World War disturbances, over Hutterite pacifism, led most of them to start migrating to Manitoba and Alberta, Canada. The identity of the three original groups which came to America has been maintained. To keep the problem of cohesion less unwieldy and to make more intensive study possible, this study has been limited to one of the three groups, namely the *Schmieden Leut'* or Smith people. The other two groups are *Darius Leut'* and *Lehrer Leut'.* On January 1, 1938, the *Schmieden Leut'* numbered 1,921 people living in seventeen communities in South Dakota and Manitoba. At the present time, May, 1939, they have eighteen colonies. The total Hutterite population in America in 1931, date of last complete census, was 3,721, living in thirty-three colonies. The total number of American colonies on January 1, 1938, was forty-eight. In addition to these there are two colonies in Europe, one in England and one in Liechtenstein. The following table shows the number, distribution, and inter-relationship of all the colonies.

### THE TIME SETTING OF THE HUTTERITE ORDER

Understanding of the Hutterites begins when one sees them and their order as a historic continuity. For in essence the Hutterite order is a continuity, a continuing persistence or constancy of a way of believing and behaving with reference to the beliefs. It is a social movement through time, a process. Much of the order has remained constant through the four centuries of their existence. Changes which have occurred have meaning as deviations or variations from the persisting pattern. The concept is the Hutterite's own. He lives not so much in the past as in a sense of identity with his cohering order, which gets its nature not primarily from present manifestations but from its character as a long continuity, from past to present. It is of the venerated, long-persisting beliefs and practices which the Hutterite thinks when he thinks of that which is most purely *Hutterische*. All the forces of the community are to be directed against deviations which might threaten the venerated central cluster of beliefs and practices. It is in the time setting that we see the first broad outlines of the pattern of Hutterite cohesion. But before more sharply focusing upon the pattern and its parts, it is necessary to give attention to another setting, the physical.

## TABLE I

### HUTTERITE COLONIES IN EXISTENCE, JANUARY 1, 1939

#### Showing the three major groups and their colonization

Colonies underlined are in the United States, all of which are in South Dakota but Montana colony which is located in Montana.

With the exception of those underlined all the *Schmieden Leut'* colonies are in Manitoba and the remainder are in Alberta.

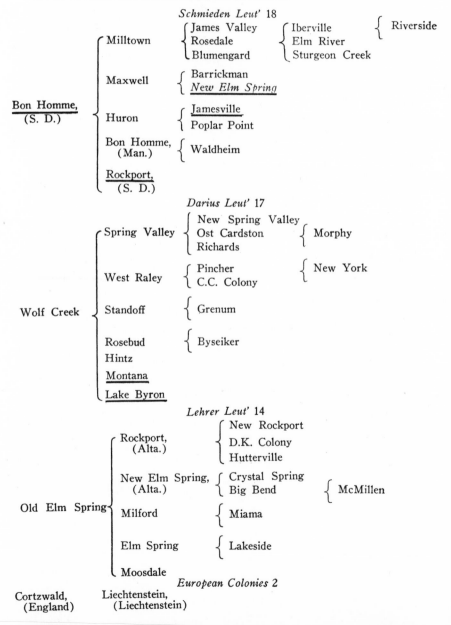

*Schmieden Leut'* 18

**Bon Homme, (S. D.)**
- Milltown
  - James Valley
  - Rosedale
  - Blumengard
    - Iberville
    - Elm River
    - Sturgeon Creek
      - Riverside
- Maxwell
  - Barrickman
  - *New Elm Spring*
- Huron
  - Jamesville
  - Poplar Point
- Bon Homme, (Man.)
  - Waldheim
- Rockport, (S. D.)

*Darius Leut'* 17

**Wolf Creek**
- Spring Valley
  - New Spring Valley
  - Ost Cardston
  - Richards
    - Morphy
- West Raley
  - Pincher
  - C.C. Colony
    - New York
- Standoff
  - Grenum
- Rosebud
  - Byseiker
- Hintz
- Montana
- Lake Byron

*Lehrer Leut'* 14

**Old Elm Spring**
- Rockport, (Alta.)
  - New Rockport
  - D.K. Colony
  - Hutterville
- New Elm Spring, (Alta.)
  - Crystal Spring
  - Big Bend
    - McMillen
- Milford
  - Miama
- Elm Spring
  - Lakeside
- Moosdale

*European Colonies* 2

Cortzwald, (England)    Liechtenstein, (Liechtenstein)

# CHAPTER III

## The Economic and Physical Environment

Unlike the literary Utopias created on paper by writers who soar in flights of imagination, functioning Utopias such as the Hutterites are definitely subject to physical limitations. The routine of living goes on in a Hutterite community like a drama subject to the physical limitations of a stage and to the physical nature of the actors. Yet the physical setting too is used in the interest of preserving group solidarity. Some physical factors the Hutterites can change; to others they must adjust. Factors to which it is particularly difficult to adjust, such as drought, are looked upon as acts of God and are accepted with fatalistic resignation. The land from which the Hutterites make their living, the organization and nature of their buildings, the physical nature of the people, even the clothing they wear, all have a relation to the community cohesion.

### THE AGRICULTURAL BASE

The fact that the Hutterites make their living almost wholly from agriculture has a bearing on their cohesion. As agriculturalists it is possible to have more of the isolation which is necessary for survival. It is possible to choose sites which are far from the disruptive influence of large cities. Experience in Manitoba, where some communities make the mistake of choosing locations close to Winnipeg, is demonstrating the disintegrative influence of the city. Almost without exception the disorganization in the Manitoba colonies varies directly with their closeness to Winnipeg. No colony within twenty miles of Winnipeg is escaping the disintegrative influence. Rosedale colony which is about fifty miles from Winnipeg is less disorganized than some a greater distance away because it is under the control of unusually strict men who recognize the dangerous influence of the great city.

9

Members of Barrickman and Maxwell colonies, closest to Winnipeg, are aware of the influence but are now little able to cope with it. It is doubtful whether there is any solution for them other than movement into greater isolation. The same influence, though to a lesser degree, can be seen at Lake Byron colony, a member of the *Lehrer Leut'*, whose members are coming under the influence of the smaller city of Huron, South Dakota. Fortunately for the Hutterites, most of their colonies have been able to choose sites which make seclusion possible.

The broad expanse of acres which surround a colony contributes to its isolation. By a survey in 1931 it was found that the average *Schmieden Leut'* community is a village of 129 inhabitants surrounded by 4,383 acres of land which they own or rent. The total value of the *Schmieden Leut'* land and property is around $1,500,000.

As agriculturists the Hutterites are able to maintain a much greater degree of unified, autonomous, self sufficiency than would be otherwise possible. When they first came to America they produced and processed almost all of the goods they consumed. They assert that the only articles they purchased outside were salt and needles. While they are steadily being drawn into our complex system of processing and distribution they still produce, comparatively speaking, a great amount of the goods they consume. It would hardly be possible for such a thoroughly communal system to be maintained in the United States or southern Canada on other than an agricultural base. At Old Bon Homme colony, which has the most remunerative non-agricultural sources of income, the cash income from non-agricultural pursuits,—grist milling, blacksmithing, woodworking, tanning and broom-making,—was a little less than $3,500 in 1929. The total cash income was $55,075.91. The total cash income of the ten other colonies, in Manitoba, in 1930, was $225,460.74 or $202.85 per capita. The total income would be much greater,—including shelter, most of their food, and part of their clothing. The people of Old Bon Homme, for example, spent in 1929 less than $1,200 or about seven dollars per capita for food purchased outside. Nearly half of this was for sugar. Some articles of apparel are still made in the community.

Wool, sheared from their own sheep, is spun and knitted into garments. In mid-June as many as fifty spinning wheels will be in operation. Leather, from their own tanneries, is used in many of the colonies to make shoes for the women and children. In 1929 Old Bon Homme colony spent $3,566.04 for ready-made clothing or about $21 per capita.

A more subtle aspect of Hutterite closeness to agriculture, difficult to define, yet emphasized by the Hutterites as important, is the natural physical setting as a harmonious setting for their religious beliefs. The Hutterites regard nature as God-made, the city as made by the hands of man. It is common to regard the city as a citadel of the devil. The Hutterites greatly enjoy their simple day by day experiences living close to nature. The physical habitat is the environment of their emotional aesthetic being as well as the physical setting of the community.

### BUILDINGS AND HOUSING

The grouping of buildings in the Hutterites community is distinctly communal and it reflects the nature of their communality. At the center is a group of buildings used in living: dormitory-like residence quarters, kitchen and communal dining rooms, bakery, laundry, kindergarten, and school. The school building serves also as church. Surrounding the central nucleus of consumers' buildings is an ordered group of barns, sheds, industrial shops, and in many communities, a flour and feed mill. A Hutterite community generally has from twenty to thirty buildings. Consumption is central in a Hutterite community, low though their standard of living is. The Hutterites have not acquired the idea that making a living is a game worthy of being an end in itself. They live to live, although the concept includes living for future life as well as the present.

The housing arrangement is a factor in the community solidarity. In a society where the individual is submerged in communal living the home is the place where individualism is most likely to appear. To the extent that the individual has privacy a person can have an *alter ego,* a more individual self within his home. There is always the possibility that the individual's loyalty to his family may be greater than his loyalty to the community and that for which the community stands. Those in authority in the Hutterite community recognize the home as a place not as easily controlled as the rest of the community. Some Utopian communities have met the problem by adoption of the practice of celibacy. Oneida community tried to meet it by abolishing the conventional family. The Hutterites meet it in part by stripping the family of many of its functions.[1] Hutterite housing is a factor in the greater submergence of the family in the community.

Hutterites are accustomed to enjoy keenly finding companionship in large groups. The home, instead of being a place of privacy, has the character of a social center. Hutterites spend evenings together in each other's homes. Social groups keep forming and re-forming. They walk into each other's homes without knocking. Residence buildings are very much like a quadrangle of dormitories. In the three or four dormitories per colony, homes are provided in each building for from six to eight households, or a total of from thirty-eight to fifty people. The average household is made up of six people or, to be exact, 5.9 as ascertained by a census in June of 1931. The number of rooms ranges from one to three and the number of occupants from one to seventeen. A household usually consists of a family. Only seven-tenths of one per cent of the *Schmieden Leut'*, thirty-five years old and older, never marry. In 1931 there were twenty-seven widowers and widows as compared with 220 married couples. The average size of the *Schmieden Leut'* family, i.e. parents or parent and children living in the same household, was found to be 6.3. Hutterite homes are kitchenless since food is served in the communal dining rooms.

The gregarious nature of the Hutterite way of living habituates them from infancy to dependence upon constant fellowship with each other in large numbers. Some have confessed that dread of loneliness is sufficient to prevent them from deserting the community.

---

[1] For a fuller discussion of this see the writer's article, "The Origins of Conflict in the Hutterische Communities." *Publication of the Sociological Society of America*, Vol. XXV, No. 2, May 1931, pp. 125-35.

A HOMOGENEOUS GROUP

The Hutterites are a homogeneous group. Although of a greatly mixed ethnic stock predominantly from southern Germany, Carinthia, and Tyrol, they think of themselves as German and more specifically as *Hutterische* German. They have a group consciousness much like that of pride in nationality. Their language is not only different from that spoken in surrounding territory but is different from other German. It is a conglomerate of words, many of them corruptions, from most of the countries in which they have lived, Moravia, Transylvania, Ukraine, the United States and Canada, superimposed upon a German base of Bavarian, Tyrolese and Carinthian admixture. Probably less than half of their speech is German.

Hutterites are very conscious of their clothing when outside of the community. For the men even the beard, which all wear after marriage, has a symbolic character marking them off from others with whom they associate. People outside stare at them and sometimes call after them, "beaver" or "buffalo" or, confusing them with the House of David, ask them about baseball. Outside of the community the Hutterite is not likely to forget his identity with the group of which his garb is a symbol. Within the community, the uniform, for such it may be called, eliminates jealousy over clothing since all are dressed alike. Men wear Quaker-like hats, black jackets fastened with hooks and eyes, and black trousers. Women wear kerchiefs over their heads, and bulging skirts of dark colors.

BIRTHS, DEATHS, AND NATURAL INCREASE

As a result of a very high birth rate and a low death rate, Hutterite population increases rapidly. By means of a colony by colony enumeration of births and deaths for the period, from January 1, 1927 to January 1, 1931, the rates per thousand population at the mid-point, January 1, 1929, were calculated. The birth rate was 44 per thousand, the death rate, 8, and the rate of natural increase, 36.[2] Since the population was only 1300 and the enumeration covered but four years the rates have only indicative value and meaning. As another means of ascertaining fertility a survey was made of the total number of children born to mothers of completed families who had husbands during the child bearing period. Seventy-five per cent had nine or more children. The mode was between ten and eleven. Thirteen per cent had from thirteen to sixteen children.

Although the death rate is low, infant mortality is high. Seventeen of the 142 children born at Old Bon Homme from January 1, 1906 to January 1, 1937, died during the first year, eleven of them shortly after birth or during the first month. Once the hazards of infancy have been escaped, the Hutterite community is an unusually healthy place. However, the Hutterites do not live to a great old age. Of the 1418 *Schmieden Leut'* Hutterites in 1931 a total of 16 were 70 or over, only one of whom was over 80.

Population increase has a number of significant relations to the community cohesion. A biologically self-perpetuating group has an advantage over the celibate Utopian communities. Indoctrination and habituation can begin early. With a high rate of natural increase, even though some communities may break up, the movement goes on apace. The thrust of population pressure keeps pushing colonies into isolation. Newly colonized groups seek greater isolation than that enjoyed by the mother community and many of them find it.

A danger arising from population increase the Hutterites meet by application of a policy. Although the Hutterites have not heard of the sociological observation that there is a quantitative limitation to the effective functioning of a primary group, they have learned from experience that a colony becomes more difficult to control when it grows beyond a certain size. It is an established principle with them that a colony should not be larger than

---

[2] The birth rate in the registration area of the United States in 1929 was 18.9 and the death rate was 11.9. The infant mortality was 67.6 deaths per 1,000 live births. *Mortality Statistics,* Bureau of the Census, U. S. Department of Commerce, 1929, p. 6. *Births, Stillbirth and Infant Mortality Statistics,* Bureau of the Census, U. S. Department of Commerce, p. 3.

150 and must not be larger than 200.   Cliques may develop within very large colonies.

In the Hutterite community one observes a highly developed adjustment of a people to their physical environment.   The adjustment suggests an organismic character.   Few opportunities are lost to utilize the natural setting in the interest of group preservation.

# CHAPTER IV

## The Central Beliefs

Within the time setting and the physical setting which have just been presented, the order coheres—but how? How the order coheres is the subject of this and subsequent chapters. The chief characteristic of the Hutterite order is its unity, the internal consistency and harmonious inter-relationship of the various parts. It is an order in a very complete sense. Understanding of the order requires discovery of this nexus of inter-relationships within. The pattern of the relationships must be more than a pattern of the moment, for in essence the Hutterite order is a long continuance or persistence through time, a social movement or process. The quest is for a pattern of inter-relationships which have persisted through the movement and which being found makes the order and its cohesion intelligible.

The unity of the Hutterite system is both the object of the present quest and a source of great bafflement. One wonders how to interpret any one category, such as religious activity, government, education, economic activity, or family life, when an adequate understanding of it is dependent upon an understanding of the relation of the part to the whole, a whole which in turn is only made intelligible as the highly fused parts are understood. The parts of the whole seems at first impression almost inseparable. The institutions of Hutterite society are but little differentiated from each other. Economic activity is a function of community government. Those who have governing authority also, by virtue of their authoritative position, administer economic affairs. There is no economic system which may be thought of as separate from government. It is a system only in the limited sense of being an organization of means of making a living in a communal community where economic activity and governing activity are merged. Education as directed by the Hutterites is

16

almost wholly an institution of the community government. It consists of indoctrination and habituation directed toward disciplining the individual so that he will conform. Much of it is informal, conceivable as education only in the broadest sense of the word. Moreover, all sanctioned activity within the community is regarded as religious. In Hutterite society, although it is a society which arose out of protest against the non-separation of church and state, church and state are inseparably one. With one exception there is no distinction within the community between sacred and secular. The concept of the secular applies only to society outside. The exception within the community is that part of the secular which, in spite of opposition, has permeated from outside.

Obviously the Hutterite community cannot be understood by making use of the familiar categories of analysis usually applied to studies of community life in our more differentiated society. To do so would be to superimpose an extrinsic conceptualization discordant to the fundamental nature of the Hutterite community. The pattern of order in the Hutterite community must be of intrinsic order peculiar to the community. There is a difference between intrinsic order which must be discovered, and superimposed order created by fiat and often called organization. Organization when superimposed by fiat can be as simple and familiar as one wishes to make it, while the delineation of intrinsic order seems of necessity to lead into complexities.

While the sacred and the secular are not differentiated within the community, there is a differentiation in degree of sacredness or religious importance of beliefs and behavior. In fact this difference, a Hutterite-distinguished difference, is our point of departure in unraveling the tangled skeins of the unity of their order. As Hutterite-conceived, it is an intrinsic distinction, a step in analysis which has meaning because it is intrinsic, a distinction emerging from the nature of their order, not superimposed upon it.

In consequence the next step in understanding the Hutterite order is a search for that which is regarded by the Hutterites as most important as revealed in their behavior. Formulations of convictions regarding fundamentals the Hutterites call the beliefs or *Die Glauben.* The problem here is an analysis of the activity of people directed toward satisfaction of what they believe to be needs and especially of activity directed toward needs regarded as of foremost importance. Needs conceived as basic, and beliefs concerning them, are focal. They are focal because definitive of lesser needs and lesser beliefs. They are a nuclear center around which the whole Hutterite society is ordered. All sanctioned activity is ordered around central beliefs, held as religious.

The concept of the central beliefs is a Hutterite one. The constantly recurring phrase, "It is *Die Glauben,*" is their incessant answer to questions as to why they do as they do. Moreover the beliefs are looked upon as traditional, persistently constant, and absolute. They are an unchanging heritage possessed from the beginning. The Great Chronicle is authoritative source as to their nature. The central beliefs are the most constant factors around which the long social movement is ordered. They serve as a frame of reference. Each new situation is defined with reference to the central beliefs. As the order has continued, each addition to it, each change, has been tested for consistency with the central beliefs. Thus they have developed and maintained an internally consistent, highly unified order.

The nature of the moving order is seen as the relationship of every aspect of the community to the central beliefs is revealed. Government, or community control, is to the Hutterites but a way of ordering living in accordance with the central beliefs. The common will which constitutes the seat of authority in Hutterite government is a common will to abide by the traditional central beliefs. Education is indoctrination and habituation directed toward developing self-discipline which will insure identification by the individual of his will with the common will to abide by the traditional beliefs. Penal discipline in the Hutterite community is an accessory to education used where educationally developed self-discipline has failed.

The total is a portrayal of the functioning order—the central beliefs concerning needs, for satisfaction of which the order came into being, and the system of means for directing the common living in accordance with the beliefs. How the order functions as an order is the explanation of how it coheres. It is an analysis of what the cohesion is, explained in terms of its functioning.

## THE NATURE OF THE CENTRAL BELIEFS—THE SUPERNATURAL SANCTION

To the Hutterites the central beliefs are preeminently religious. The beliefs are regarded as expressions of the will of God. Thus supernaturally sanctioned they are held as absolutes. About their ultimate rightness the Hutterite feels absolutely certain. Since the Hutterites system is ordered around the central beliefs, the rightness of the system too is held with absolute certainty. The Hutterites assert with profound conviction that they have "the one right way." The absolute certainty which the Hutterites possess is a factor of prime importance in the cohesion of their order. The conviction that their system is supernaturally sanctioned and is absolutely right is described by them as their most important belief. This belief, unlike the others of their central beliefs, concerns their assumed relation to Deity rather than their direct relations to fellow man and as such is strictly religious. As a result of this belief the regulative authority in the community is regarded as derived from and validated by the mind of God. The Hutterite way with all of its compulsions is viewed as unquestionably right because vouched for by omniscient Deity. To question such rightness so established is held as sin.

The role of absolute certainty in the cohesion of Hutterite society and in the integration of their personalities is significant. By possession of absolute certainty a basic need for security is satisfied. To the Hutterite, security is much more than economic. With a feeling of complete resignation to the will of Deity, a characteristic outside observers often describe as fatalism, the Hutterites have a remarkable sense of security even in the face of poverty and death. According to Hutterite doctrine one wins protective approval of Deity through suffering and martyrdom. One is concerned with the security of life after death. Yet it would be over-simplification to interpret Hutterite religion as primarily a desire to go to heaven or to escape hell. The attitude is one of extreme dependence. In the case of the Hutterites, it is dependence not upon a personal God intimately thought of as a father, but upon the absolute authority of Deity. With his absolute certainty the Hutterite escapes much of the hazard of living inherent in the difficulty of making predictions in social situations. Living involves activity, activity leads to necessity to make choices, and choice-making has within it the hazard that one may not choose wisely. The Hutterite escapes much of the mental tension which arises from apprehension regarding the effect upon the future of choices made. He does not expend energy in doubting. All of his choices which might be difficult are pre-determined. They are determined not by ministers and elders primarily, but for ministers, elders, and all the members alike, by supernaturally sanctioned, traditional beliefs. The only task is uncompromisingly to interpret the present situation with reference to the central beliefs. Then no matter what happens, an omniscient and omnipotent power will take care of one. There need not be anxiety in times of crisis for beneath are "the everlasting arms."

The Hutterite's possession of absolute certainty leads him to have an authority-centered mentality. Accustomed to accept authority as the chief, in fact almost the only, way of knowing, he submits to discipline with remarkable facility. He is accustomed to lean and to be directed. Regulation, which would seem like regimentation to others, is not very irksome.

The authoritarian attitude makes critical thinking unnecessary and thereby protects the system. Critical thinking, if directed toward the central beliefs, would undermine the system. When a Hutterite, due to outside influences, begins to think critically about his way of living, he is headed for mental conflict and, unless he stops this kind of thinking, for desertion. After desertion, according to the testimony of deserters, he never again knows the deep peace he had while living in the community. Since critical thinking is not only unnecessary, but if widely practiced, would destroy the system, the Hutterites discourage it. Education for critical thinking is not part of Hutterite pedagogical procedure. They regard it as dangerous to the *status quo*. With spurring mental tensions absent, the Hutterite is content to get along without critical thinking and whatever might be produced by it.

THE NATURE OF THE CENTRAL BELIEFS—A UNIFIED CODE OF LIVING

Important though the supernatural sanction is with its provision of absolute certainty, religion to the Hutterites is primarily a way of community living. For that living their beliefs provide them with a unified, all-inclusive code. Unlike our society, Hutterite society has but one code. Unlike Middletown, where people are pulled in opposite directions by antithetical beliefs, the Hutterites find their beliefs a focalizing center for the social harmony of their community and the integration of their personalities.

The nature of Hutterite central beliefs and the relation of the beliefs to the supernatural sanction is shown in the following quotation from a printed leaflet containing a petition made by the Hutterites to President Woodrow Wilson in 1918. It is given at some length and quoted directly because there is a revealing quality in the Hutterite's own expression of their attitudes. For four centuries they have been willing to go to their deaths rather than deviate from their constantly held beliefs.

"The fundamental principles of our faith, as concerns practical life, are community of goods and non-resistance. Our community life is founded on the principle, 'What is mine is thine,' or in other words, on brotherly love and humble Christian service, according to Acts 2:44,45: 'And all that believed were together, and had all things common; and sold their possessions and goods and parted them to all men, as every man had need.' . . .

"Our community life is based on God's word, and we could not serve God according to the dictates of our conscience if we were not permitted to live together in our communities. Our members would, by the help of God, suffer what He may permit, rather than consent to leave the community life. . . . The Church . . . must conform to the express teaching and example of the Master.[1] She is in the world, but not of the world.

"Our history is written with blood and tears; it is largely a story of persecution and suffering. We have record of over two thousand persons of our faith who suffered martyrdom by fire,

---

[1] In the petition the Hutterites add that they regard outside "government as ordained of God for the reason that not all men are followers of the meek and lowly Savior."

water and the sword. Our Church has been driven from country to country, and rather than compromise their principles, have fled to various countries until at last they emigrated from Russia to this country in 1874. . . .

"We humbly petition our Honored Chief Executive that we may not be asked to become disobedient to Christ and His Church, being fully resolved, through the help and grace of God, to suffer affliction, or exile, as did our ancestors in the time of religious intolerance, rather than violate our conscience or convictions and be found guilty before our God."

The central beliefs of the Hutterites are: (1) that their way of living is sanctioned by omniscient Deity who must be obeyed, even to martyrdom, (2) that it is the will of Deity that they live communally, (3) that it is the will of Deity that they practice non-resistance, and (4) that they must live simply, avoiding the outside world, in it but not of it. The first, obviously religious in character, concerns their assumed relation to Deity, while the latter three, religious by virtue of assumed dictation by Deity, concern relations to fellow-man. The latter three are beliefs which when accepted without supernatural sanction, could be organizing principles of secular groups. These latter three, secular when assumed without supernatural sanction, are what the Hutterites call principles of practical living. In actual behavior it is the principles of practical living which are most central. Aside from the supernatural sanction, the central beliefs around which Hutterite behavior is ordered, might, from the standpoint of outside values, be viewed as secular. Therefore, aside from the supernatural sanction with its cohesive factor of certainty, the pattern of Hutterite order is a secular pattern subject to sociological analysis.[2]

---

[2] The usually offered explanation that the Hutterite and other Utopian communities cohere because they are religious, is not adequate. It is necessary to ascertain the operating pattern of order which the group assumes to be supernaturally sanctioned. Religion is commonly offered as the explanation because religious Utopian communities have survived much longer than non-religious. It has been possible to ascertain with quite a high degree of accuracy the dates of origin and end of 130 Utopian community systems in North America representing 244 separate communities. Of these, 35 systems representing 125 communities were avowedly religious and 95 systems representing 119 communities were non-religious. Ap-

There are many evidences in Hutterite behavior that principles of practical living concerning social relationships are stressed more than assumed personal relation to deity. For three and one-half centuries, i.e., since their system reached the institutional stage, the Hutterites have not sought mystical religious experience. The Hutterite system is organized around authority revealed in the Bible and in their own chronicles. The Hutterite attitude toward Deity is one of extreme obedience to and respectful veneration of an omniscient, omnipotent, protective authority. They do not have intimate, personal communion with Deity. God is referred to as "Father" but the term is severely patriarchal in character bespeaking the dignity of relationship between subject and sovereign patriarch. Prayer "goes through the clouds to God." Prayer is ritualistic, not personal communion. Mechanically recited prayers are offered daily in religious meetings, before and after each meal, and in the morning privately in the home. Private prayers are almost always recitations which have been learned in "German school" or in church. In times of crisis prayers are petitions to benign authority for special aid. Only the singing in religious meeting suggests emotional catharsis, and then by the women. The Hutterites like to sing. It is one of their few means of self-expression. There is no evidence that the Hutterites turn to communion with Deity for companionship or satisfaction of the wish for response. They find their need for response and companionship abundantly satisfied in their gregarious, communal living.

The Hutterites explain their worship ritual in a way which may be described as habituation and indoctrination. They say, "The

---

proximately one out of every two non-religious systems failed the first year while only one out of 10 religious systems failed in that time. Only one out of every 33 non-religious systems survived as long as 25 years, while at least one out of every two religious systems has survived 25 years or longer. No non-religious systems lasted 50 years, while one-fifth of the religious systems have. Several religious systems have continued over a century. The Hutterites with a longevity of over four centuries, and still thriving, are of course patriarch of them all.

Based upon a study by the writer reported at the annual meeting of the American Sociological Society, December 1931, under the title, "American Idealistic Community Experiments." The writer is indebted to Julia Williams for technical assistance in revising these data and bringing them up to date. The original source material may be found in her Master's thesis, *An Analytical Tabulation of the North American Utopian Communities by Type, Longevity and Location,* University of South Dakota, 1939.

plant must be watered each day." With surprising, naive insight they state that their consciences are community products. "We are brought up from so high (indicating the knees) to believe as we do." "My conscience was trained from childhood."

Formal practices concerning man-to-Deity relationships are not extremely stressed. A Hutterite may stay away from a religious meeting with impunity, although few do. Having a guest is sufficient reason for not going to church. He may work on Sunday if it is considered at all necessary. The mills are often run on Sunday when there is an unusually large grist to put through. A Hutterite may omit grace at meals when outside the community, although most of the older ones pause to recite a brief, silent prayer before and after the meal.

Theological concepts are colored by the way of living, as well as having an influence upon it. It has been pointed out that in this authoritarian society the concept of God is primarily a concept of absolute authority to whom one gives submission. Obedience is more important than worship. The Hutterite is most obedient who most conforms. "Only your will you have to give up," is a constantly repeated statement in a Hutterite community. The Hutterites speak of God as *"unsichbar"* (unseen). "God is so bright and holy we can't look at Him." They emphatically insist that they do not think of Deity as personal. When trying to describe his concept of Deity a minister stated, "If your father were a millionaire and he said to you, 'If you don't do anything against my will, you will have my property,' wouldn't you do his will?" Yet this economic illustration was used as an explanatory device to make Hutterite thought intelligible to an outsider. Heaven is not thought of as a place of economic wish-fulfillment. There are no pearly gates, and no streets of gold. Hutterite heaven is not a place for conspicuous consumption. Except at times of cruel torture, the Hutterites do not look upon heaven as a place to which to escape. Heaven is vaguely conceived as like a perfect Hutterite community where everyone conforms to the ideal *Hutterische* way. No threatening outside world surrounds it. It is an idealization of the present community order projected into the future. The Hutterites say they fear Hell, and the thought that they would go to Hell if they deserted the community is a cohesion-producing factor, but fear as a sustained emotion is incongruous in such a non-neurotic society. Hutterites live more for rewards than to escape punishment. Hell is pictured as a place of eternal heat and hot pitch forks.

The chief points in the foregoing are: (1) that in the central beliefs the Hutterites have one all-inclusive social code. (2) This code is religious because assumed to be supernaturally sanctioned. (3) In actual behavior the Hutterites stress the central beliefs as "principles of practical living" in the community; to the Hutterites religion is primarily a way of living and the central beliefs are primarily beliefs about how to live. (4) The ethical and non-mystical character of their beliefs is shown in their attitudes toward worship and in their theology. The central beliefs are primarily secular principles unified by supernatural sanction.

#### THE ROLE OF CONSCIENCE

The Hutterites talk much of the will. The individual must give up his will. All in unison must submit to the will of God. When trying to persuade a person from outside to join the community, the Hutterites say, "Living in community (i.e. under communism) is not hard. Only your will you have to give up." Certainly the identity of the individual will with a common will is a factor of paramount importance in the cohesion of the community. The effective sovereignty, the seat of authority resides in the common will of the group. It is a common will to be loyal to and abide by the traditions. As long as there is a unified common will unimpaired by threat of individual deviations, the community system is secure.

Will has a seemingly anomalous character in the Hutterite community. They frankly look upon it as a product of community training yet regard the act of willing as autonomous and significantly so. Great stress is placed upon the autonomous character of the act of willing. After the individual has been carefully indoctrinated and habituated for approximately the first eighteen years of his life, he is called upon voluntarily to will to be baptized and officially join the group. Baptism is a ritual signifying that the individual has publicly willed to give up his will, to merge his individual will with the common will of the group. It is the most important event in the life of the Hutterite. The assumed autonomous character is significant. Each individual assumes that of his own volition he submits to the central code. Thus the common will is no group entity but an aggregation of the wills of individuals each of whom regards himself as willingly supporting the code with his loyalty. Since all individual wills are directed toward sustenance of a common code, the aggregate is a common will.

Of foremost importance in the process of making sure that the will of the developing young Hutterite will become one with the common will of the group is the operation of conscience. As previously pointed out, conscience too is definitely regarded as a product of community training. Little children are thought to be not as responsible for their mischievous acts. Their consciences have not yet been fully developed. Even twelve year old children are only half-Hutterites. It takes about eighteen years to grow to a full-fledged Hutterite ready for the sacred rite of baptism.

The Hutterites define conscience, as "the thing which tells you when you do wrong," "getting scared inside when you do wrong," or "how you feel inside when you do wrong." "Wrong" is any prohibited act of non-conformity. Foremost wrongs are acts which do not conform to the beliefs in pacifism, communism, and simple living. It is wrong, or sin, to hold back money from the community. Such an act is defined as theft. It is an unpardonable sin to put on a military uniform or give any kind of military service. It is wrong to take oath, vote, or hold political office outside. Going to law is considered wrong, but the Hutterites have done it many times since coming to America. It is wrong to smoke, to drink liquor to the extent that one becomes intoxicated, to have one's picture taken, to possess or try to play musical instruments, to have a radio or listen to a radio, to shave after getting married, to wear clothing other than that provided by the community, to attend motion pictures, dance, gamble, or indulge in "sparking" (courtship). Not all wrongs are of equal seriousness and consequently not all are avoided with equal conscientiousness. The seriousness of a wrong tends to be determined by the Hutterites' trial and error experience in determining the seriousness of the threat to the central beliefs and the coherence of the system. Some practices, such as the use of hooks and eyes on their black jackets, instead of buttons, the Hutterites observe solely because they are folkways or customs.

While the Hutterite knows that his conscience was developed in him as a result of his environment, he looks upon it as a controlling authority which he must obey. "My conscience wouldn't let me," is looked upon as sufficient explanation for all conformity. The Hutterite obeys his conscience because fear makes him uncomfortable when he does not. His emotional equilibrium is dependent upon following the dictates of his conscience. Conflict is distressing. True, group pressure would be brought to bear upon him if he did not conform, but in most situations he can be depended upon to discipline himself in accordance with his community-grown conscience. Conscience is of great significance as a means of self-discipline, making discipline by the group rarely necessary. At the center of the Hutterite system is individual will merged with the common will and self discipline made possible by the development of a community-developed conscience in conformity with the common will.

The Hutterite community is fundamentally religious because the Hutterites regard their beliefs and their way of living as supernaturally sanctioned. As a result of the conviction that the order is underwritten by Deity as absolutely right, the Hutterites are sustained by a profound certainty regarding the central and most important values in their order. They have one all-inclusive code which is free from conflicts. The system, organized around central beliefs, came into being, (1) as a means of escape from tensions during the revolutionary period known as the Protestant Reformation, and (2) as a means evolved from trial and error experience, for satisfying needs. The central beliefs are the most constant factors in the Hutterite order. They serve as a frame of reference with regard to which each new changing situation is defined. Thus all parts of the order have an internal consistency. The chief sources of authority for ascertaining what is regarded as the will of God, are the Bible and the Hutterites' own historical records known as the Chronicles. The Great Chronicle serves as a constitution, a hand-book for living in accordance with the code, and, through its record of martyrdom, an inspiring source of loyalty.

Social behavior is emphasized more than personal worship. The Hutterites have a community-centered religion. As supernaturally sanctioned, observance of the rules of social behavior brings a satisfying sense of the approval of Deity, and assurance of going to heaven and of escape from hell. Beliefs held as central are derived from an interpretation of the Biblical ideal of brotherhood plus a supporting doctrine, derived from pre-Reformation asceticism, that simple living and avoidance of the world is virtuous. Faith in the latter doctrine protects the system from disintegrating outside influences.

Loyalty to the central beliefs is assured through the operation of conscience. By means of conscience, consciously inculcated in the individual from childhood, the Hutterite is trained for self discipline which assures that his individual will, will be merged with the common will to abide by the supernaturally sanctioned, traditional beliefs. The system is an authoritarian one. It is regarded as being based upon traditional beliefs sanctioned by the will of Deity. Operating authority within the community resides in the common will of the members to abide by the beliefs. How the common will operates is the subject of the next chapter.

# CHAPTER V

## The Pattern of Government—Organization of Authority

### AUTHORITY IN COMMUNITY CONTROL, ULTIMATE AND DELEGATED

In the preceding chapter it was shown that central beliefs are focal in the Hutterite system and that the Hutterites have a common will to live in accordance with the central beliefs. The subject of the following two chapters is the organization of means through which the common will of the group functions. The first concerns the organization, nature, and principles of authority as a means of general administration of community activity. It might be called the administrative structure of Hutterite government. The second concerns the disciplinary functions of those in authority in the Hutterite community; education for self-discipline and the exertion of pressures as a means of penal discipline. Chapter VI might be called the disciplinary functions of Hutterite government. In an authoritarian society such as the Hutterites, discipline in one form or another is the chief function of community government.

The concept of authority is central in the organization of means for living in accordance with the beliefs. Authority exercised by the Hutterites is ultimate and delegated. Ultimate authority is held by the group which expresses the common will. Such ostensibly is the voting group made up of baptized males. It is an adult group, since baptism does not occur before the age of eighteen and usually not until the age of twenty. Included in the ultimate authority, though not admitted as such by the Hutterites, is the power held by the women who, due to their more sheltered living, exert a conserving, tradition-conforming influence of great importance. That ultimate authority resides in the common will of the adult group is demonstrated in two ways. (1) Historically, when the common will has weakened, the communities have suffered serious disintegration. When many individual wills deviate from the traditional common will, the system weakens and the members lose their power to act concertedly.   (2) It will be seen that all administrators are elected by and are answerable to the electorate and those who influence the electorate.   On occasion, administrators have been deposed from office for failing to conform to the traditional common will.

Delegated authority is vested by the members in two groups, one regarded as especially religious and having highest administrative authority, and the other regarded as having authority limited to the business of making a living.   The first is made up of the minister, the assistant minister, when a community has one, and a group of elders or trustees.   The second is made up of a business manager and his heirarchy of assistants.   The business manager is directly subject to the authority of ministers and elders.   In most communities he is one of the elders.

Administrators act with delegated authority vested in them by the voting group.   Their responsibility is to enforce the common will, and administer business affairs.   It is assumed that the common will is a traditional, common will ascertainable by consulting the chronicles as well as by consulting the members.   The chief duty of the administrators is to prevent deviation from the common will.   Conservatism is a foremost quality demanded of an administrator.   Administrators are selected (1) for their orthodoxy, which means their dependability, in carrying out the traditional central beliefs, and (2) for their probable ability as business administrators.   This is in keeping with the emphasis in the Hutterite community upon developing followers rather than leaders. The more specific nature of the groups having ultimate and delegated authority will be next considered.

### HEADQUARTERS

A Hutterite community is managed by a group of elders or trustees who are presided over by the minister.   The Hutterites refer to this central administrative group as "headquarters." Subordinate to the minister and under the direction of "headquarters" is a person who handles the money and manages. the work organization.   In German he is called *haushalter* and in English by the misleading term of "boss." Recently some Hutterites have preferred to call him by the more accurate term of "business manager." "Headquarters" is made up of from four to seven members most of whom have other important positions in the community. The group always includes the minister and the business manager and almost always the person next in authority under the latter, the "farm boss." Half of the *Schmieden Leut'* communities have assistant or "second" ministers and in such communities he is a member of the board of elders. The assistant minister is responsible for discipline and formal indoctrination of the youth in "German School." Generally all of the most important functions of the community are represented by men on the board of elders. Administrative authority is centralized in the minister. In some communities he dominates the elders and thus the whole group, but always his dominance is restricted to the limitations set by the traditional beliefs.

The chief duty of the members of "headquarters" is to determine and direct policies. The members of "headquarters" must make sure that the policies will have a safe consistency with the traditions and that policies will be voluntarily supported by members of the community. They do the latter by "talking up" policies among the members and by showing that such policies are in conformity with the traditions. Those in authority know that the strength of the community depends upon voluntary loyalty of the members. It is recorded in the chronicles that in times of disorganization a multiplication of rules was of little avail. The minister and other members of headquarters know that the power they wield is not centered in themselves but in the common will of the group, a will to conform to the traditional beliefs. Hutterites all, administrators and those administrated, are prisoners of the past. Their government is essentially a system of means for ordering living in accordance with a persisting pattern of traditional, central beliefs.

The chief responsibility of the minister is to make decisions, since not all decisions are referred to the elders or the electorate. He also must decide which decisions to refer. The minister is an interlocutor interpreting the present with reference to the past.

To do so he must be well informed about Hutterite history and is in part chosen for his familiarity with the chronicles.

The tenure of office of all members of headquarters is for life on good behavior. The Hutterites assert, "We don't change headquarters. That makes our government better." However, several ministers have been removed from office. William Roublin was put out of office and out of the community for keeping back twenty gulden for his private use. Sigmund Schulte was "sent to the devil," i.e. excommunicated, for "selfishness." He too accumulated private property. George Saunrich was excommunicated for not reporting to the elders the adultery of his wife. Matthias Hofer, a fanatic, was excommunicated because he "went too far" in strictness. He demanded that prayers be offered loudly and in concert both before and after midnight, that no Hutterite work for wages for a non-Hutterite since the latter might profit from it, and that Hutterites must not sing while at work.[1]

Members of headquarters are elected. Ministers are chosen carefully. In the *Schmieden Leut'* colonies when a minister must be chosen, the members of headquarters in the community concerned first ascertain opinion in their own community and other communities of their *Leut'* as to who of the local members would be the four best nominees for the office. Nominees are then announced, and voted upon by the baptized men members of the community concerned. Voting is done orally. Then the name of each candidate who got five or more votes is written on a piece of paper, which is placed, name down, in a hat or a box. The oldest candidate draws one of the pieces of paper out of the receptacle. The name thereon is the name of the newly selected minister. The Hutterites state that in the last step God guides the hand of the one who draws the name from the hat. One skeptical member has asserted, "I should think that God could choose as well from all, but this is our custom. Sometimes the one who received the least number of votes is the one whose name is drawn." This method of selection permits the elders to make sure that a reasonably capable man will be chosen, at least one of

---

[1] Johann Loserth, "The Decline and Revival of the Hutterites," *Mennonite Quarterly Review,* April 1930, Vol. IV, pp. 105-6.

the four most capable, satisfies members of all the other colonies of the *Leut'*, permits the voters to have a part in the selection, and by ritual gives the "election" and the one selected the authority of supernatural sanction. The drawing by lot also reduces the possibility of ill-will over the election. And with characteristic practicality the Hutterites make sure that God does not make a serious mistake. After a few months of probation the newly selected minister is ordained by "laying on of hands" by two other ministers. Elders and more important administrative officers are chosen by direct vote of the baptized members. Lesser administrative officers are appointed by headquarters.

Under the general supervision of headquarters is an elaborate work organization administered by the business manager or *haushalter*, usually called "the boss." Directly under him are a farm boss who supervises most of the work of the men, since most of the duties are agricultural, and a kitchen boss and garden boss who supervise the work of the women. Under the farm boss are a large number of appointive positions. At Old Bon Homme colony these include a cattle boss, a horse boss, a sheep boss or shepherd, a hog boss, an assistant or "second" hog boss, a chicken boss, a duck boss who also has charge of the geese, an island boss and an assistant island boss. Except for the latter two, who supervise work on Bon Homme island in the Missouri River, the organization at Old Bon Homme community is little different from any other Hutterite community. Other occupations include first and second miller, blacksmith, carpenter, tanner, shoemaker, and broom-maker. Usually the minister serves as bee-keeper. With the exception of the minister-apiarist, men in the latter positions are directly responsible to the business manager. The only women with fixed occupations are the kitchen boss or head cook, the garden boss, and two to three women who alternate in managing the *kleine schule* or day nursery and kindergarten.

All of the able-bodied women of the community come under the supervision of the kitchen boss, in work rotated week by week. At Old Bon Homme colony when the population was about two hundred, thirteen women washed dishes for a week every third week, eight to ten women milked cows for a week every third week, and two women assisted in the kitchen and two in the bakery every twelfth week.  All women able to work gathered for potato peeling daily.

When there is urgent seasonal work to be done in the fields, all able-bodied persons in the community, including the minister, but excepting the cooks and kindergarten supervisors, come under the emergency jurisdiction of the farm boss.  Thus the community has a mobile labor force always available to meet seasonal demands. The Hutterite penchant for thorough and minute organization is a factor in the effective order of the community.  There is little lost motion in the flow of authority, from minister to stable boy.

The authority of the chief administrators in a Hutterite community is subject to checks, with the result that those in power cannot easily exploit others by use of it.  All money is handled by only one member, the business manager, who is under strict surveillance of minister and elders as well as the eyes of fellow members who associate intimately with him.  Administrators are subject to the same communality as the rest of the members.  They have no better homes, clothing, or food.  There would be little opportunity for consumption of personally acquired wealth, were it acquired.  Men in authority are largely removed from temptation to exploit their authority to gain prestige.  The Hutterites do not recognize superiority of status of administrators as administrators.  Hutterite boys do not aspire to be the minister or a boss.  Men prefer to escape administrative responsibilities but accept them when requested.  In the Hutterite community it is a sin called vanity to seek superiority of status.  The greatly stressed success pattern in our culture appears to the Hutterites as a form of frenzied foolishness.

### THE SOVEREIGN COMMON WILL

Ultimately, administrative authority rests upon the common will of the adult members.  The members express their will formally through the vote and informally by voicing their opinions.  Only the men vote.  All Hutterites, men and women, express opinions on occasion.  In the Hutterite community it is almost impossible to differentiate between the formal and the informal methods of democratic expression. Voting on matters of policy is almost as informal as mere expression of opinion. The chief difference is that only men vote. The informal process of "talking it up," as the Hutterites state it, is recognized as more important than the matter of vote taking. Evidence of this is shown in the following description by a minister of a general business meeting of the voters. "I put up questions to the members. If anybody is against it, he is to say so. They talk it up in small groups. If the (whole) group gets quiet, then it means, 'yes.' I can tell by the quietness whether they are for it." In the talking-up process the elders are busy. If there was unanimity among the elders when a matter was first talked over by them in council, it is highly probable that there will be unanimity among the members when it is presented in the general meeting.

However, sometimes one of the small groups, which form like ephemeral eddies in a stream, may become a nucleus of a definite movement. From such nuclei changes in policy emerge. It usually takes many years of talking before a minority wins the majority to support its position. It took many years of informal discussion to win for women the right to wear sun bonnets. A long time was taken to effect a change in the "gates" of men's trousers. For some years the question as to whether colonies should own automobiles has been in process of discussion. Hutterites will blandly announce that in a few years a certain change will take place because it is being well talked of now. Some predict that eventually buttons will be substituted for hooks and eyes on men's jackets. The button clique and the hook-and-eyes clique discuss it jocularly, but it is such discussion which ultimately determines policy. Danger to the community lies in secretive issues too contrary to the central beliefs to permit open discussion. One such is the desire of parents for more spending money with which to buy dolls, candy and toys for their children.

The chief function of the members in expressing their common will is, however, not so much in initiating new policies as in checking authorities from deviating from old ones. Authorities are selected to administer in conformity with the traditional beliefs. It is when they obviously deviate that the common will of the group is asserted as ultimate authority.

Hutterite men stoutly, but nevertheless erroneously, assert that the women have no part in running the community. Women do not vote, hold office or attend business meetings. One exception where the men grant that the women have a controlling responsibility is in the preservation of the sex mores. Women are told that the sex morals of a community depend upon them. "If the women are good, the men will be good and if the women are bad, the men will be bad. Adam was driven out of the garden of Eden because Eve was tempted and didn't use good judgment."

The attitude of the men toward the women is definitely patriarchal. The women are told not to talk in public "because they don't know enough." "St. Paul said, 'keep still in meeting.'" When a former Hutterite leader was asked why the doctrine of brotherhood does not include equality of women with men, he replied, "Yes, we are all equal, men and women, in the eyes of the Lord, but the husband is the head of the wife, so we rather take the head than the feet."[2] Women are sheltered as a matter of policy. Except for annual trips of the young women to other colonies so that they may be selected for marriage, women in South Dakota colonies rarely get out more than once every year or two. Women are almost always silent in the presence of strangers and non-members. Sheltering of the women does much to keep them conservative, i.e. closely attached to the existing order of things.

It is significant that in the Hutterite community, organized as it is around a traditional pattern, the women are more strict in adherence to the pattern than are the men. Sovereignty in the Hutterite community lies in more than common will; it is in the common will to abide by the traditional beliefs. The will of the women to abide by the traditions is more strongly fixed than that of the men. The powerful, indirect influence which they exert upon the men, and thus upon the community, is great because they are submissive. Their submission is not so much to the men as it is to the traditional way of living. By their more complete surrender they exert a strongly conservative, steadying influence in the community. While the women do keep still in meeting,

---

[2] "The Diary of Paul Tschetter," *Mennonite Quarterly Review,* July 1931, p. 215.

they talk things over with their husbands in the privacy of their homes at night. They censor their husbands' behavior when the latter deviate from the straight and narrow path. Women supervise the private lives of their husbands,—that very small realm left which escapes the vigilant eyes of the rest of the community. One Hutterite husband testifies, "Modern scholars don't believe in heaven and hell. I had some of those books but the Mrs. threw them out." Women are also closer to the children of more impressionable age. It is admitted by the Hutterites that some ministers are greatly influenced by their wives when making decisions.

Submissiveness to traditional authority accounts for the influence of the women. It is the same submissiveness which contributes to the ultimacy of authority held by all adult members. The strength of the community depends in great part upon the degree to which the individual surrenders his will by identifying it with the common will. The Hutterites do not recognize nor appreciate the conserving role of the women.

The functioning Hutterite order is organized around the common will of the adult members, directly and ostensibly around the common will of the men voters, and indirectly and unadmittedly around the still more conforming common will of the women. The common will is a will to live in accordance with traditional, central beliefs regarded as essential for satisfying needs. The voting group officially delegates authority to administrators. The chief responsibility of administrators is to determine policy, always with reference to the central beliefs; supervise the business of making a living; and guard the community against dangerous nonconformity which would threaten the system and therefore the group's security. The agencies used for guarding the community against non-conformity are primarily disciplinary, training for self-discipline, and penal discipline by the group.

# CHAPTER VI

## THE PATTERN OF GOVERNMENT—DISCIPLINARY FUNCTION

### THE NATURE OF HUTTERITE DISCIPLINE

Control in the Hutterite community is based upon a long-established principle that "if you let the child get started when little, you can't hold him when big." "As soon as you let go on one thing, there is another thing." The Hutterites express their first principle of control with the incessantly repeated phrase, "Don't give them too much rope." Fundamentally it is a principle of prevention. Non-conformity, the Hutterite equivalent of what would be crime and delinquency in our society, must be checked at its inception or before. The functioning of the principle includes a two-fold program of control.

The two chief means of control are education for self-discipline and penal discipline by the group. The principle of prevention operates in each; the effectiveness of each is dependent in large part upon its effectiveness as a means of applying the principle. Through education the individual is trained for self discipline. Penal discipline is regarded as supplemental to education, to be used where education has failed. To the extent that self-discipline is achieved, penal discipline is unnecessary. The Hutterites have little faith in coercion as a means of control. It is not only disharmonious with their basic belief in non-resistance, it has also been found inadequate. The Hutterite order does not have the precarious kind of stability which is maintained by coercion.

### THE NON-HUTTERITE SCHOOL SYSTEM

Not all education in the Hutterite community contributes to cohesion. There are two educational programs in each community, one which has been forced upon them during the past few decades by states and provinces in which they reside, and the

38

other, a program which is their own. The superimposed system has a bearing here as an influence which the Hutterites are trying to counteract. For the two programs are antithetical and in direct conflict with each other. Within each community a battle is being waged on an educational front between two widely different social orders, their own and ours.

It is no less a battle because in part being waged unconsciously. The Hutterites, especially those in Manitoba, are only partly aware of the threat to their order of the standard school system. In Manitoba, where the community members cannot select their own teachers and have no authority over them some members say, "Yes, the person whose bread I eat, his song, I sing." But many of them agree with their fellow-member who said, "I can't see any effects. If it affects any, it would affect my children and I can't see any." It seems significant that in Manitoba Hutterites were declared disqualified as trustees of their schools and that most of their schools are under the highly centralized control of one trustee employed by the province and responsible to the Minister of Education. He employs and discharges teachers, determines salaries, levies school taxes, and has full authority to direct policies. Teachers are not deliberately encouraged to try to disorganize the colonies. Moreover, after a first unsuccessful attempt to force the Hutterites to fly the Union Jack and place pictures of the king in the school rooms, coercion was given up as a method. But if better education of the Hutterite children leads to their ultimate Canadianization, Manitoba officials will not be averse to it. They are now content to await the operation of a long-time policy of handling the Hutterite minority group.

In South Dakota the conflict between clashing educational programs is even more unconscious in its operation, and effects of the superimposed system are less noticeable. The state department of education and the various county superintendents of schools have no definitely formulated, concerted, plan to Americanize the Hutterites. The first outside teacher to be employed by the Hutterites was voluntarily brought in by members of Old Bon Homme in 1909. The minister regarded her as having

a "worldly" influence upon the girls and discontinued the practice.   Recently a Hutterite woman said of the first school teacher,
"She taught us about one hundred songs and we know every
one of them yet.   Singing is surely the nicest thing in the world."
In 1921 the state legislature passed a law requiring that all
schools in the state be taught in the English language.   In all
of the colonies some English was being used in the schools
before that date.   In order to get school funds amounting, for
example, to about $500 annually at Old Bon Homme, the whole
elementary school program had to be taught in English.   More
recently, requirements concerning certification of teachers have
become stricter with the effect that no *Schmieden Leut'* colony
now has a qualified member who may teach.[1]

Altogether, twelve Hutterites from the three major groups,
*Schmieden Leut', Darius Leut'* and *Lehrer Leut',* have been sent
out of the community for advanced education to prepare them
as colony teachers.   Seven went to Dakota Wesleyan University
at Mitchell, South Dakota, and two to a normal school in Calgary,
Alberta, two to an Alberta high school, and one each to Huron
College, Freeman Junior College, and Springfield Normal School
which are located in South Dakota.   One who went to Dakota
Wesleyan also took two courses at Northwestern University.
The experiment was regarded as unsuccessful since only one, a
man in Alberta, now qualifies as a teacher.   The last two who
were sent out "got to dancing and doing that stuff" and as a
result the policy has been definitely abandoned.   The Hutterites
say, "It takes a very strong constitution for a man to go out."

The scope of the English school has been rather steadily
increased.   At Old Bon Homme, pioneer in this field, a low
quality of fifth grade work was initiated in 1912-13, sixth grade
work in 1915-16, and seventh grade work in 1926-27.   Up to
1931 no *Schmieden Leut'* member had entered the eighth grade
and only nine were in the seventh.   Most of the adult Hutterites
have had no higher than an inferior sixth grade eduation.   Many
of them are little more than literate in the English language.

---

[1] The standard English school is taught by a Hutterite in only one of the
forty-nine colonies in America.   He secured a first grade certificate after
taking normal school training in Calgary.

The Hutterites assert, "You don't need an education to be a farmer."

The superimposed school system is already having noticeable effects particularly through the personal influence of the teachers. Teachers have introduced outside songs and competitive games. Some teachers who live in the Manitoba colonies have radios. It is against the rules for children to listen to the radios, but they do and as a result develop increased interest in the outside world and its luxuries. A few Hutterite boys have radio crystal sets which they manage to keep hidden from the authorities. Teachers talk of adventurous interests in the world outside and stir up restlessness. Some of them, by making education interesting, awaken a desire for more education. In Manitoba, teachers have introduced some boys and girls to the vast world of recreation and self-development to be found in reading books and magazines. One Hutterite girl fell in love with a school teacher and left the colony to marry him. Teachers introduce new foods and stimulate the Hutterites to seek a higher standard of living. Even the better clothing of the teachers is believed to awaken desire for better dress and thus cause discontent and vanity in the youth.

Hutterite objections to the standard school program tend to be stereotypes defined with reference to the central beliefs. They think that the teachers make the young people "worldly," that physical drill is too much like military drill, and that there is too much emphasis upon war in history text books. Some Hutterites criticize our teaching of history as an attempt at patriotic indoctrination. Hutterite children get their lowest grades in history, yet they readily learn the history taught to them from the Chronicles in the "German school."

As a result of the conflict in educational programs, Hutterite children are beginning to be pulled in two ways. The development is too recent to be of great significance yet, but the battle is on. The enemy is within the gates, operating upon the most vulnerable part of the community, making use of the most powerful weapon which can be used upon them. The Hutterite program of education for self-discipline is being put to a test. The

Hutterites are handicapped because there is no precedent recorded in the Chronicles to which they may turn for guidance. The Hutterites are not adept at meeting new situations not definable with reference to the Chronicles. Were they to follow the pattern set in the Chronicles they would move to a new frontier.

### EDUCATION FOR SELF DISCIPLINE

The Hutterites depend upon a variety of means for training their members. Some means are organized into institutional form and some are not. Some apply only to children while others apply to the whole group. Formally organized means are, a kindergarten, a school of religious indoctrination called "German school," and a daily religious meeting called, "church." All are carried on in the Hutterite German language. Informal means are as diffuse and inclusive as the whole community itself.

The kindergarten exists as a group means for early indoctrination and habit training. In the American colonies it is attended by children between the ages of two and one-half to five. The two contemporary European colonies place children in the kindergarten at the age of six weeks. In the historic Hutterite colonies of the 16th century it was attended by children between the ages of one and one-half years to six years of age. Most of the year, attendance is from nine in the morning until four in the afternoon; in summer it is from eight to five. Children are taught prayers, verses from the Bible, and hymns, and a few nursery rhymes. Food is served mid-morning and mid-afternoon. Hutterites assert that it takes only half as much food to provide the children when they are in kindergarten as it does when they are fed at home. Although the kindergarten is a traditional institution, it has been abandoned by some of the colonies in recent years. Members of such colonies say they have not sufficient room, but less charitable members of other colonies say they are getting "too lax." Of the eleven colonies in 1931, five, in Manitoba, had no kindergartens. The average attendance where kindergartens still continue was fourteen. One of the most important influences of the kindergarten is habituation to the gregarious, communal way of living. Children spend most of their waking hours in a group of ten to sixteen of their own age where co-operative relations are emphasized and competitiveness is severely suppressed.

Children under the age of five are only vaguely aware of the great world outside of the community. It is a place from which feared strangers come, speaking an unknown language. Between the ages of five to six, children sit in at the English school session to acquire a little familiarity with the unknown language by hearing it spoken. At this point of first effective exposure to the influences of the outside world, indoctrination in Hutterite beliefs becomes important. The "German school," attended by children from five to sixteen years of age, exists for that purpose.

"German school" too is a traditional institution which has been undergoing changes. It is mentioned in the Great Chronicle as early as 1533. From early Hutterite documents it is possible to learn something of the Hutterite school system in the sixteenth century. The writer of one, and probably of both, of the documents was the Horace Mann of Hutterdom, Peter Scherer, also known as Peter Walpot. Schools then were like boarding schools in which children ate and slept, as well as attended classes. With characteristic Hutterite emphasis upon detail and organization, much attention was given to minute instructions to teachers regarding child rearing. Emphasis was placed upon not allowing the child to become "self-willed."[2]

The contemporary German school is like a blanket of counter-indoctrination thrown around the English school session. It is usually held a half hour before and a half hour after each session of the standard school. The children are taught prayers, hymns, a catechism, and are given instruction in submissive, co-operative behavior. The catechism, a printed pamphlet, is organized with questions and answers which are learned by rote. All recitation is done in unison. Even instruction is not individualized.

The daily church service is an important part of the Hutterite educational program, of which hymn singing is probably the most

---

[2] "A Hutterite School Discipline of 1578, And Peter Scherer's Address of 1568 to the Schoolmasters." Translated by Harold S. Bender, *Mennonite Quarterly Review,* Vol. V, October 1931, pp. 231-245.

influential. Hutterites express most of their emotions in song, sadness as well as joy. Indoctrination and emotions of martyrdom are stressed in Hutterite hymns. Many are rhymed Bible stories. Some are doctrinal, presenting the accepted views on communism, pacifism, baptism and communion. Some offer solace. The great majority are stirring songs of martyrdom, many of which contain lengthy accounts of early tribulations. These, as all Hutterite hymns, are sung through, a line at a time, first by the minister and then by the congregation. Many of the hymns were written in prison. Although the most productive period of song writing ended about 1570, the Hutterites still turn to writing songs in times of crisis. A number were written by men confined at military camps during the world war. Melodies are very seldom original. Some are adaptations of pre-Reformation religious songs and others are based upon folk songs current in the sixteenth century. "Little Flower on the Heath" is a favorite melody. Early songs were gathered together and published in 1914 at Scottdale, Pennsylvania in a book of 894 pages entitled, *Die Lieder der Hutterischen Brueder.* An abbreviated edition containing 525 pages was published in 1919. The influence of hymns upon the Hutterites can hardly be overestimated.

Indirect influences upon the Hutterites include countless daily acts of exemplary behavior, particularly co-operative behavior, and what the Hutterites call the *"Gemeinsinn"* or community spirit. A community has a pervasive *Gemeinsinn"* which must be preserved. The Hutterites assert that the character of the individual is largely a product of the community influence. They try to keep the influence effective. Although much of the Hutterite educational procedure is not formally organized, it is highly unified. Its effective unity is derived from clear-cut definition of objectives and from the non-conflicting nature of Hutterite central values and beliefs. The Hutterites know precisely what they wish to teach, for the qualities of "good" community membership are clearly defined. The home, the Hutterite educational program and the community influences do not confront the child with conflicting standards. In this freedom from inner culture conflict the Hutterite community differs significantly from our society.

The chief objective of Hutterite education is the achievement of self-willed or voluntary conformity. The stress is upon self-discipline. The Hutterites frankly regard education as a means of preserving the status quo. Education for critical thinking is seen as a threat to the order, and is avoided. Basic beliefs are viewed as settled and lesser beliefs are consistent with them. The Hutterites regard it as inconsistent to seek preservation of the status quo and at the same time to emphasize "free enterprize." Anything springing from individualistic, as opposed to communal, interests is viewed as non-conformist or what in our society would be called, "subversive." When the individual is indoctrinated to feel that he autonomously supports the established order, a penal discipline by the group is little necessary and sustaining loyalty is assured. The Hutterites recognize that loyalty is a state of mind which cannot be produced by coercive commands.

In consequence the educational methods used by the Hutterites are training of the emotions rather than the intellect, and indoctrination and habituation. Emotions are developed to react positively in the direction of spontaneously given loyalty. This is done by emphasis upon history, martyrdom and the use of hymns. Emotions are developed to react negatively as conscience, the nature of which was discussed in an earlier chapter. By means of habituation and indoctrination the Hutterites achieve automatic responses of action and thought. Whether the colony in which one asks a question be in South Dakota or Manitoba, the answer is likely to be the same and given everywhere in almost identical words. Such results are in part accomplished by incessant repetition.

### PENAL DISCIPLINE

There is comparatively little non-conformity in most of the Hutterite communities because culture conflict is not great. Since culture conflict arises almost wholly from outside influences which penetrate, misconduct requiring penal discipline varies directly in accordance with the extent to which a colony or an individual has come under the influence of our society.

In the colonies which are close to the traditional pattern, and this includes most of them, offenses requiring penal discipline usually are not serious in nature. Boys may smoke, throw stones through windows or at the fowl, smuggle Jew's harps into the community, or stray off the colony grounds. Although phenomenally rare, they may get to quarreling among themselves. One delinquency problem has an unusual character derived from the communality of the community. In our culture it would be called theft. In a society where all property is common, a child has a limited opportunity to learn the meaning of the concept, private property. He gradually comes to learn it as his knowledge of the outside world increases and as adults prepare him for adjustment to it. To most Hutterite children there are but two kinds of property, common property which is available to them and common property which is not available because it is kept locked up. The latter includes candy in the store-room. In consequence articles may be taken from the cars of visitors or from the residence of the school teacher when there is opportunity. The Hutterites punish such offenses. Girls get into much less trouble than the boys. They break the less strictly enforced rules against decoration of the person or of one's room.

Means of control of adult members who err range all the way from friendly private admonition to excommunication. If a member sees another breaking one of the lesser, enforced rules, it is his duty to speak to the erring brother. If the latter mends his ways, no other steps are taken. If he continues to offend or if his offense is of a serious nature, such as holding back money from the community, it must be reported to the minister. According to rigorously observed Hutterite ethics, it is the duty of all members to be informers regarding the behavior of each other.[1] If an offender does not reform after being admonished by the minister, he is required to appear before a week-day eve-

---

[1] On one occasion a Hutterite got into the writer's notes and copied parts of them in an attempt to get evidence about a suspected member. When queried about the ethics of his behavior he was greatly grieved and pointed out that it was his moral duty to do it.

ning religious meeting and ask forgiveness of the members, after which he is given public admonition. If, now a recidivist, he still continues, he is required to appear before the Sunday morning religious meeting in daylight. If all of the series of graduated pressures are of no avail, he is excommunicated. This means that he is socially isolated from the community. His whole world turns against him. He must eat alone. No one may talk to him. He is treated as if he were not a member of the community. After a week or ten days of such treatment most members reform. Those who do not reform, find life in the community unbearable and leave. The Hutterites get rid of their irreformable recidivists by expelling them into our society. Such drastic outcome occurs very rarely.

When penal procedure becomes emphasized in a Hutterite community it is weakening. The continuance of the order depends upon voluntarily given loyalty to the central beliefs. Through the centuries, even through two periods of great disorganization when the communal way of living was held only as an unattainable ideal, the Hutterites have managed to continue perpetuating that loyalty. When conditions became too difficult they have migrated into the isolation of new frontiers. Now two influences, unprecedented in Hutterite experience, confront them, namely a superimposed educational system and the subtly penetrating influences of modern technology. To deal with these they cannot turn to the chronicles for guidance. If disorganization becomes so great that it threatens the survival of the system, as it does in two or three colonies, they may have difficulty finding a new frontier. It is probable that the ability of the Hutterites to continue may eventually depend upon whether they can find a more isolated frontier and whether they will have sufficiently escaped dependence upon the comforts and conveniences of modern technology to be willing to move into it. It must be borne in mind that with their present rate of natural increase, a hundred survivors could populate quite an area in a few generations. Frontier or no frontier, if those who live outside the Hutterite colonies continue to persecute them, as it has been the human pattern to do intermittently for four centuries, the long continuance of the Hutterites is likely to be assured.

# CHAPTER VII

## Technology Comes to the Hutterites

Pressures from outside the community which make martyrs of the Hutterites contribute to cohesion; most other outside influences threaten it. In addition to the super-imposed school system the foremost outside influences threatening the community are related directly or indirectly to the broad category of technology. Very early in South Dakota the Hutterites began adopting machinery and other instrumental devices from the world outside. Some colonies which moved to Manitoba have come under the influence of Winnipeg.

Hutterites get most of their contacts with the world outside through trips and association with visitors. Some colonies subscribe to a newspaper and a magazine or two, usually *The Pathfinder,* but few members read them. Most influential contacts are secured through trips.

In most of the colonies few trips are made outside. At Old Bon Homme where the amount of outside travel is much like that of the other *Schmieden Leut'* colonies in South Dakota, the young men get out approximately ten times a year. This includes trips made to other colonies to find a wife. Men between the ages of twenty to seventy make about twenty trips a year, chiefly on business. Permission must be secured to make trips, and records are kept stating names of persons making them, date, and place of destination. The purpose of record-keeping is to give all an equal chance and to control the more adventurous. A few men, called peddlers, chosen for their ability to sell community products, make from thirty to forty trips a year. Men over seventy years of age get out from six to seven times a year "just to see what the world is like." Women and girls rarely go out of the colony and then primarily for medical services or to visit other colonies. Usually a wagon load of girls from Bon Homme is taken each year on a visiting tour to other colonies "so the young

48

fellows can see them." Such trips are exciting events. Girls will boast, "I know the whole gang at Rockport and at Jamesville." After a girl becomes married she is not likely to leave the colony grounds more than once every two or three years. Many of the old women have not been out for a great many years.

Nearly half of all trips made by Bon Homme people are to Tabor, a village eight miles away, or to Yankton, a city of approximately 6,000 population, nineteen miles away. Over eighty per cent of trips are made to small places within thirty miles. If to these are added trips to other colonies and to a Mennonite clinic at Marion Junction, ninety-five per cent of all trips are accounted for. Most of the other five per cent are to small places within one hundred miles.[1] Each year usually two young men from Old Bon Homme spend the winter among Manitoba colonies. They usually come back with a wife, and with new ideas. The number of trips made by members of Manitoba colonies and the effects of them will be discussed shortly under the topic, The Influence of Winnipeg.

THE MARCH OF TECHNOLOGY IN SOUTH DAKOTA COLONIES

Technological influences in South Dakota colonies have largely been limited to the adoption of machinery and similar instrumental devices. Since 1875, a year after coming to America, there has been a progressive march of technology in the colonies. A steam-powered mill was built in 1875 at Old Bon Homme with the help of men from Amana Society. In 1880 a portable steam engine was purchased by the same colony to displace horse power in running the threshing machine. The first gasoline engine was purchased in 1905 by Milltown colony, at a cost of $299, to be used to saw wood. The following year Huron colony purchased a large gasoline engine. In 1907 Old Bon Homme bought a large gasoline engine and a tractor for plowing. Records at Old Bon Homme show that expenditures for engine fuel and lubricants

---

[1] Notable exceptions are trips made by ministers. During 1936-37 two Hutterite ministers, one from Old Bon Homme, toured western and central Europe to inspect the colonies in England and Liechtenstein and to visit historic Hutterite sites.

were trebled in two years after purchase of the first engine and quadrupled in six. In 1916 a Fairbanks Morse diesel engine was purchased for use in the Old Bon Homme mill. Subsequently all colonies have purchased tractors and a great amount of farm machinery to be run by them. Large caterpillar tractors are now most commonly used. No farm in surrounding territory is as mechanized as a Hutterite community. Many Hutterite men are skilled mechanics. Most of them enjoy working with machinery.

The first telephone was installed in 1910, at Old Bon Homme. Some years of discussion preceded adoption, for the innovation was vigorously opposed. The adoption was justified on the grounds that one telephone connection with the community was needed in emergencies to save life and to make possible early reception of telegrams from other colonies. Liberals pointed out that it was asking too much of neighboring farmers to expect them to bring in messages. Now the Hutterites say, "It all depends upon how we *use* it. It is no sin to have a telephone." The Hutterites continuously and very definitely make a clearcut distinction between two aspects of what the anthropologists call our "culture." One is that part of our "culture" which is viewed as means to ends and which may be adopted if used strictly for Hutterite ends, i.e. in conformity with Hutterite central beliefs and values, and the other concerns the more ultimate values held in our society. It is the latter which the Hutterites strenuously seek to resist. The definiteness of this distinction cannot possibly be overemphasized. It provides the Hutterites with what they regard as a justification for adoption of instrumental devices from our society. The Hutterites quite universally express themselves with stereotyped phrases and the stereotype in this situation is, "It all depends upon how you *use* it." The Hutterites regard it as safe and "right" to adopt our instrumental or technological "culture" as long as they use it "right." "Right" use means use which is *believed* not to threaten the system or more specifically what the Hutterites call "the beliefs." Under no circumstances must the more ultimate values of our society be adopted if they conflict with the Hutterites' own. Such is "worldliness," a form of heresy signifying that a community is becoming lax.

Electricity was introduced in the Hutterite communities in 1912 at Maxwell colony. Most of the colonies which moved to Manitoba have since adopted use of it. In some colonies the Hutterites assert that it costs less to have a community generating plant than to buy kerosene for lamps. It has been customary to install electric lighting first in shops and barns, then in dining rooms and school, and finally in the residence buildings. Thus technology creeps up on the Hutterites. Devices introduced as producers' goods tend in time to become consumers' luxuries. Old Bon Homme resisted use of electricity until 1929 when it was used only to light the mill. In 1937 they installed a generating plant to provide power and light for the mill, and light for shops, barns, dining rooms, and school. Installation of electricity in the residence buildings at Old Bon Homme is still opposed.

The first automobile came into use in 1928, at Old Bon Homme. An old model T Ford was rented to be used in great emergencies such as necessity to take an acutely ill person to a hospital. In 1929 the writer found the residents of Old Bon Homme agog over the automobile. They liked to talk about the mechanical advantages of the late models they had seen at Yankton. The hands of young mechanics, skillfully trained to repair tractors and other machinery, itched for the automobile. One member stated, "If I didn't live in community I'd get myself a big Stutz and pass you and wave goodbye at you." Systematic questioning revealed that the automobile was desired more than anything else which might be adopted from the world outside. Members were beginning to feel that it was a downright hardship to live under a system where the automobile was denied. After some years of discussion, opinion had developed to the point where action was necessary. Yet at the same time Hutterites were fearing unknown possible consequences of adoption of the automobile. They were saying, "Automobiles cause trouble. A trouble at Amana is the automobile. Young people go out in cars and don't come back." By the summer of 1930 the conservative minister at Old Bon Homme acquiesced and a used Ford was purchased for sixty dollars. All solemnly agreed that it was to be used only in emergencies and for special business purposes, not as a luxury. However, a nearby neighbor observed, "They all want to drive it." Ownership of the car was justified by pointing out that they were paying almost as much rent for a car each year as this one cost. And always one heard, "It's not a sin to have a car. It all depends on how you use it." After purchasing the automobile, Bon Homme members sat back in some trepidation to watch the reaction in other colonies. Manitoba colony members asserted, "Bon Homme is too much out in the world." But a little later a Manitoba colony purchased an automobile. They protected their consciences by offering it for sale shortly after purchase. The price was set high and it seemed good economy to use the car until sold. They are still using it. Meanwhile Old Bon Homme has purchased another car and a couple of trucks.

### THE INFLUENCE OF WINNIPEG

However it is the influence of the large city of Winnipeg which is most immediately disorganizing. Most of the Manitoba colonies are scattered over an area of fifteen miles diameter just south of the Assiniboine River about half way between Winnipeg and Portage la Prairie. Distance from Winnipeg of colonies in this group varied from eighteen to thirty-two miles, airline. A few other colonies are fifty to sixty miles south west of Winnipeg. The number of trips being made to Winnipeg and the state of disorganization of the colonies varies with striking directness with their closeness to Winnipeg. At Barrickman colony, closest to Winnipeg, many of the boys were getting to the large city as often as one hundred times a year. Most of them were leaving without permission, taking a chance on "catching Hell" when they got back. Adult men were averaging forty trips a year. Men and boys at Maxwell, only two miles farther away, were getting to the city but slightly less. Those at Iberville, about seven miles more distant from Winnipeg, were making a large but correspondingly less number of trips. In all of these colonies the girls were still getting out but rarely. The girl who made more trips than any other girl of the *Schmieden Leut'* was getting to Winnipeg but three or four times a year. She explained, "I'd like to go oftener but you know how it is. You have to wait your turn." Rosedale colony, fourth in closeness to Winnipeg, about twenty-seven miles from it, was an exception due to a policy of unusual strictness held by managers who were aware of what was happening to the colonies close to the city. Fewer trips were made from Rosedale and the colony was more conservative but not as much so as the colonies fifty or more miles from the city. At Huron and New Bon Homme colonies, farthest of the Assiniboine group from Winnipeg, adult men were making but six to eight trips to Winnipeg per year. Boys and girls were rarely getting out. At the colonies fifty or more miles from Winnipeg not more than a trip or two a year was being made to Winnipeg by the adult men, and practically none by the boys or girls.

The largeness of the city of Winnipeg is a significant factor in its attractiveness and influence. In the Assiniboine group, the colonies which are farthest from Winnipeg, a city of 218,000 in 1931, are closest to the small city of Portage la Prairie with a population of 6,600. Yet the colonies which are escaping much of the influence of Winnipeg because far from it are not conspicuously coming under the influence of the smaller city eighteen miles away. A man at Barrickman colony describes the influence of the great city as follows.

"The trouble here is that there are no small towns or cities near us. The city we have to deal with is a very large one. In South Dakota only small towns and cities were near us. The effect of small cities is much different from the effect of a large city. Trips to a city like Scotland or even as big as Huron were not bad for the colony.[2] When the young people come home from Winnipeg they feel bad. They say they have seen so many things they would like to have and would like to do and they feel that because they are colony people they are denied all these things.

"Yes, it is undoubtedly true that the colonies which are farthest away from Winnipeg have the least trouble. But then, too, there is management. Managers who are strict and who do not let the

---

[2] However Lake Byron, a *Lehrer Leut'* colony twenty miles north of Huron, South Dakota gives evidence of more disorganization than any other South Dakota colony. Since the colonies concerned were of the *Lehrer Leut'* the writer did not attempt to determine why colonies which have been near Huron have usually become more disorganized than colonies near Mitchell, a city of about the same size.

young people get started in their enthusiasm for the city have the least trouble. But the managers do not like to deny their young people.

"We have had ten times as much trouble in the thirteen years here than in the forty-three years in South Dakota. One thing leads to another. First it's one thing, then it's another thing. First they go to movies and run around the streets. That leads them to other city ways. Music leads to dancing. The city makes them want money and they steal to get it."

Even at the more strictly managed Rosedale colony there is the same pessimestic note. A member at Rosedale stated:

"We know that our members go to Winnipeg too much. It gives them the modern world feeling. It breeds too much into them. They copy the style, especially the young boys. Style is endangering our religion now. They try to live as close to the border as possible. They seem to be a little ashamed of what they are. They get so far away from the religious. The youngsters of fourteen to eighteen seem to be ignorant of the whole thing. They don't take time to think. But they do seem to have a conscience."

On the other hand members of the more distant, isolated communities look with much disapproval upon their erring brothers near Winnipeg. One of them has said, "I tell them in the face, 'I can't tell you from a Winnipeg man.' "

As the foregoing quotations have indicated, the effects of Winnipeg are manifest in desire for money and for more worldly clothing and living conditions, and in influence which the Hutterites describe as style. The Manitoba Hutterites sum up the situation with the phrase, "One thing leads to another." The specific nature of the effects of Winnipeg and of the processes of disorganization involved will next be noted.

"Money is the greatest danger," one hears Hutterite authorities say. Hutterite expressions of opinion indicate that they look upon desire for money as dangerous because insatiable and because as a result of it inequality and divisiveness appears. They have not given enough thought to the subject to think of it as also involving the clash of two different economic systems. Hutterites in South Dakota have said: "Our religion has nothing to do with (does not provide for having) money. Money would divide us up. If people have a little money they want more. You know a little food makes a big appetite." "It's because everybody has the same that we don't have jealousy. If one had more than another that would start trouble. The *Lehrer Leut'* are rich and they think they are better." "It happens to the boys. They wish money. But we watch that; we kill it out as soon as it happens. Money and idle time are bad."

Since coming to America the Hutterites have adopted the practice of issuing a small amount of money to members when trips are made to a city or village. The amount per person is usually twenty-five cents. At Old Bon Homme, for example, the average head of a family has an annual cash income of about five dollars, depending on the number of trips he was able to make. The money is usually used to buy candy, cookies and trinkets for the children. One parent at Old Bon Homme has remarked, "It's hard to keep money around the house when you have children."

As an attempt to curb "stealing," i.e. taking colony property or withholding earnings, one Manitoba colony tried issuing a larger amount of money. Regarding the experiment a member said, "It didn't work. There is no end to what a person wants. To give them more money was to incite their cityward desires." Another Manitoba colony has permitted what might be called an invasion of capitalistic principles into their communal order. Families at James Valley are permitted to own geese, usually ten in number, from which they may sell eggs and feathers for private gain.

Desire for money ultimately leads to lack of industry. The Hutterites refer to it as "loafing." Young men in the more disorganized colonies have been heard to say, "Why should I get out to work. I don't get paid for it." Each one tends to look critically at the other and to scale down his own output of work accordingly. A man in his early fifties will be heard to say that he is getting too old to work. Laziness in the Hutterite colonies when it appears is definitely a product of the influence of our society. Hutterites in most of the colonies are industrious, conscientious workers. There is no problem of laziness. The fact, pointed out in chapter one, that the Hutterites are solvent, self-supporting tax payers in an area where much of the population is on relief, seems sufficient evidence.

Stealing, as defined by the Hutterites, is a problem in many of the colonies. A few members manage to get a little money surreptitiously by trapping animals, making articles for sale, or selling colony wine, watermelons or other products of the community. It is in colonies near Winnipeg or which have been near Winnipeg that the problem has become more serious. Hutterites assert that in 1930 a member of James Valley colony was arrested and sentenced to three months in jail for selling a load of colony wheat. In June of 1931 a member of Milltown was arrested for forging a check for $9.50 against his colony. On January 28, 1939 a charge was filed against two Hutterites and a person outside by the minister of Jamesville colony which had recently migrated from Manitoba to South Dakota. The charge was theft of approximately 195 bushels of barley valued at $55. This resort to outside courts which began in 1930 is a serious indication of disintegration for it reveals Hutterite lack of faith in their own means of penal discipline. Problems are likely to increase as long as colonies continue to be exposed to the attractions of a large city and young people say, "I like Winnipeg if I have money there."

By "style" the Hutterites mean the modernity which some members are seeking. It usually refers to clothing and to home furnishings. Style, too, is more of a problem in Manitoba than in South Dakota. In South Dakota one hears a Hutterite girl wistfully say, "Outside the ladies have nice clothes. Here we wear only dark, but the ladies who come here on Sundays (to look at the Hutterites) wear pink and white and light clothes, and flowers." Some girls in Manitoba near Winnipeg have gone beyond the wistful stage. "It's old fashioned not to have silk stockings." Most of the deviation in clothing style for women in a Hutterite community occurs underneath the uniform, somber garb required of one as a member of the community. Hutterites have a way of professing ignorance about deviations difficult to control if such deviations are out of sight. A Hutterite girl asserts about a few of her friends who wish to be modern, "We wear bloomers. Girls outside don't even wear bloomers." The standard garb of a Hutterite woman is two or three petticoats. More daring Hutterite girls wear only one petticoat in winter and none in summer. One girl declared that she has rayon pajamas and announced, "I feel as if I hadn't been aired for a week if I sleep in my underwear." Accepted practice is to sleep in one's underwear, which for women is a slip of gingham. One of the more intolerable offenses of the Hutterite girls, practiced by not more than one or two, is to visit the home of a friend in Winnipeg and put on the completely modern dress of our society just to have the experience. When a Hutterite deserts his colony, as a comparatively small number have, one of his first acts is to get other clothing. Sometimes he ceremoniously burns his old uniform.

In two or three of the colonies the young men too are becoming more stylish. Their deviation is more overt, more obvious. They shave their necks and sometimes get their hair cut by an outside barber. Some of them have trousers with creases in the proper place, brightly colored hosiery, gay sweaters, watches with chains, neckties, and caps instead of hats. None of these are permitted in the strict colonies. However, even rather conservative adult men in the more disorganized colonies are shaving their necks and trimming their beards.

In a few Manitoba colonies Hutterite homes are blossoming out. Barrickman colony is distinctly modern. At Iberville the painted chests and furniture have been moved upstairs. "It is old style." The new style is natural wood waxed or varnished. Some colonies have flower gardens. A few families have potted flowers. In the colonies near Winnipeg one may see such articles as hand mirrors, hair brushes, wash bowls and pitchers, ornamental table cloths, rocking chairs, cretonne and lace curtains, and pictures on the walls. Barrickman has an upholstered sofa and a Congoleum rug. Professional photographs of two young men may be seen on a dresser. Wall paper is used in one colony.

All of the Manitoba Hutterites have departed from the practice of sleeping on feather ticks in summer. They have mattresses. In summer, mattresses are placed on top of the feather ticks and in winter the position is reversed. Conservative colonies in South Dakota do not deviate from the established custom of sleeping between or on feather ticks. In some of the Manitoba colonies one also sees bedspreads, embroidered pillow cases and patchwork pillows.

A rather definite cycle may be noted in the influence of Winnipeg upon Hutterite personalities. Contacts there awaken desires which cannot be satisfied in a community which emphasizes communal, rather ascetic living. As desires are awakened which are unsatisfiable within the community, the Hutterites, particularly the youth, seek to acquire money, and it must be done illicitly. Rules are broken. Communal property is purloined. With the flaunting of some rules others become questioned. Young people become critical of authority and ask, "Why have so many little rules? We all break them." The authoritarian character of the order comes under questioning. The appropriation of communal property for private use leads to more individualistic attitudes. Individuals begin to think in terms of "I" instead of "we" and "my" instead of "our." The practice of communism itself becomes questioned. The questioning of one central belief leads to questioning of another. Old sustaining certainties become shaken. The validity of the whole system which makes it necessary to dress differently and live differently becomes questioned. At this stage the Hutterite, pulled between two worlds, no longer knows the old peace which was once his. He becomes a person without a culture he can call his own. The deep peace which is the chief creation of the Hutterite world is no longer his. The seemingly fuller living of the outside world which pulls him cannot be his unless he leaves his faith and his people. Frustrations be-devil him. Tensions make him unhappy. He no longer even looks like other Hutterites. Desertion seems the only solution but fear of Hell now becomes poignant for from childhood he has been taught that all Hutterites who leave go to a place of eternal torment. Conscience, once a sure guide, is now a tormenter. Finally the choice seems clear; continued discomfort in the colony or a break to the alluring world outside. Not all Hutterites who leave go through this process which the writer has observed in case studies of a few individuals undergoing it. Some young men leave for a temporary jaunt into the outside world and a few of them stay out. But the Hutterite who leaves with full intent to break with his world goes through a period of disequilibrium quite out of harmony with the deep placidity which prevails in most members and in most communities. Placid members, for a fleeting moment lose a little of their placidity when they think about the future and their old age. "When the foundation is out on one side, the house leans."

# CONCLUSIONS

Returning to the problem of cohesion with which this work started, what has been said? First it must be pointed out that social analysis of the Hutterite communities illustrates the nature and complexity of the concept of social causation. Where interaction exists explanation of cohesion cannot be an enumeration of "causes." Factor *a* affects *b* and in turn is affected by *b*, and *a*, thus altered, reacts upon *b*. In a continuum, which point or points shall be selected out as causes? The answer seems to be that explanation is presentation of the pattern of interaction of relevant factors in the whole. The pattern of Hutterite community cohesion is presented in fullest form in chapter IV.

The persistence of this cohesion pattern is of particular interest not only in itself but also in its relation to understanding the community structure. A community, a social movement, or a social order lends itself particularly to the case history method of investigation. In this approach one must avoid the temptation to think of the group as they are at the moment to the exclusion of their nature as a developmental whole. In thus viewing a situation one can see significant differences in the relative constancy of various parts of the order. Some factors are long enduring, persisting throughout the life of the order. Others are ephemeral deviants which gain meaning by comparison with the persisting factors.

Briefly stated, a social order such as the Hutterite's is a way of living and believing which came into being to satisfy needs and is organized around the satisfaction of these needs. The core of the Hutterite structure is an ideology or a set of beliefs which defines the objectives around which the system is ordered and which are held by them to be of foremost importance. Each new situation which the Hutterites meet is defined with reference to them. As each adopted change in the community is met by testing for consistency with the central beliefs the whole order in its continuance tends to maintain the strain of consistency which so greatly accounts for the holding together of the Hutterites. Social movements have been organized around many kinds of objectives. One which, like the Hutterites, is organized around common interest in satisfaction of a large number of needs is most likely to survive.

In the Hutterite communities the central beliefs are viewed as supernaturally sanctioned and thus as absolutely right. The supreme certainty which the Hutterites possess is an important factor in their freedom from conflict and their holding together. Security to the Hutterites is more than economic; it is certainty regarding life after death and certainty of supernatural protection in all emergencies.

Observing the pattern more fully one sees that administration and control in such a community is a system of means for ordering living around the cherished beliefs. Authority resides in a common will to abide by the beliefs. Education is a process of indoctrination, habituation, and stimulation of loyalties designed to develop sufficient self-discipline to insure conformity to the common will. The Hutterites have discovered the effectiveness of self-discipline as a means of control. It is a basic factor in the coherence of their order. As a result of it the order depends little upon precarious coercive discipline. It is of much significance that as a result of ordering their system around clearly established central beliefs the Hutterites have one all-inclusive code. With the exception of the comparatively few deviants who have come under the influence of our society the Hutterites are not pulled in conflicting directions. In the communities where outside influences increase and they lose this source of order, disintegration sets in. A prime necessity for the Hutterite order and perhaps for any social order is clear definition of objectives. A culture organized around antithetical values obviously lacks stability. Under a clearly defined inclusive code, government becomes less cumbersome, education becomes oriented, and crime and non-conformity unacceptable to the group becomes very much less. Yet with emphasis upon the common will and self-discipline the Hutterite government is not dictatorial. A focal problem facing the educator in our society is "education for what?" The Hutterites have answered the problem for themselves. Their educational process is effective because oriented in a system with clearly defined objectives. Hutterite experience demonstrates that the extent of crime in a society is closely related to the degree to which the society is free from culture conflict. They also have an effective method of treatment of "crime," namely prevention made possible by having clearly defined non-conflicting central values. In passing, it may be noted that Hutterite experience also demonstrates that people will work industriously without reward of private gain and that competitiveness is not essential for the long continuance of a system. The fact that the Hutterites are so completely communal and thus free from jealousy and divisiveness is a prime factor in their continuance.

There are other factors related to Hutterite community cohesion. The homogeneity of the group is a factor in their "we-group" consciousness. The Hutterites have discovered that the face to face, primary group character of the community cannot readily be maintained if a group becomes larger than approximately two hundred. Distinctive clothing, difference in speech, difference in customs, everything which makes them conscious of being a group apart, contributes to consciousness of kind within the group and consciousness of difference from people outside. A very high rate of natural increase insures against population decline due to desertion. Isolation has been necessary for Hutterite survival. Possibly an idealistic order having the size of a great nation would find isolation less necessary although evidence from European nations of censorship of outside influences seems to point to the contrary. The Hutterites secured isolation by repeated migration to new frontiers. The agricultural character of the community has made possible greater isolation and autonomy. The pressure of persecution producing martyrdom has been a force of outstanding importance in Hutterite unity and survival.

Many problems and productive problem areas remain. The student of religion would find much to investigate in the Hutterites' quest for certainty and in the Hutterites' concept of the role of the supernatural. The non-competitiveness of the Hutterite system is a challenge to further study. A very productive study might well be focused upon the experience of the adolescent in the Hutterite community. It is upon him that most of the controls are most intently directed. Evidences of community disorganization first become manifest in him. Anthropometric measurements to ascertain possible effects of inbreeding and desertion would be interesting. Those who think of unlimited peace as a desirable ideal would find value in studying this group which has achieved a high degree of peace and harmony at the cost of freedom from tensions which stimulate.

# VITA

Lee Emerson Deets was born in Emerson, Illinois, May 4, 1898. He was graduated from Sterling, Illinois, High School in 1917, received the A.B. degree from Northwestern University in 1921 and the M.A. degree from Columbia University in 1924. From 1921 to 1926 he was engaged in part-time social work in New York City. From 1926 to the present, with the exception of a two year leave of absence to continue work in sociology at Columbia University, he has taught sociology at the University of South Dakota, head of the department since 1931, at present with the rank of Associate Professor. In addition to teaching, his chief activity in South Dakota has been research and participation in the development of the social work program of the state. He has read three papers on the American Utopian communities before sections of the American Sociological Society and was president of the South Dakota State Conference of Social Work during the year 1935-36.

# EPILOG

# EPILOG

Peacefulness and order stand out in greater contrast now in the Hutterite communities. The big change since 1939, which turned out to be something of a pivotal year, has come to us. Perhaps a next study of the Hutterites should take on a larger and more difficult whole, namely what can be learned about social order by comparing the two cultures, theirs and ours. In our world outside the Hutterite communities a difficult conceptual problem on the highest level of theoretical abstraction has become everyman's nitty gritty practical problem, source of no little anxiety. A Louis Harris poll made for *Time* in 1970 announced that 85% of the people in the United States, a very high percentage in a poll, "wanted desperately to find orderly change."[1]

Such a study would do well to look for generic principles common to both their small-group *Gemeinschaft* kind of order and our modern complex organization. It is not a question of choice of either-or; the human race cannot go home again to *Gemeinschaft*. Although Ferdinand Toennies referred frequently to the early extended family when discussing *Gemeinschaft*, it sounds no little like a Hutterite community.[2] Basic in it are systematized social values which the religious Hutterites, for reasons which will be discussed later, prefer to refer to as beliefs, and a common will (wesenwille) which emerges out of associating together as compared with a rational will directed toward a specific purpose. A mechanism through which naturally emergent will operates is conscience. Common interests are put above individual interests and the individual tends to be subordinate to the group. The mental climate is more affective than rational. Tradition and the mores tend to dominate. However the order is self-created and self-perpetuating dependent on what might be called two inners, the common will within the community and internalization of that will in the individual as conscience. The order is little dependent upon laws of a state superimposed from without. Toennies acknowledged indebtedness to Sir Henry Maine's earlier work on status and contract. Emile Durkheim discussed this societal form under the caption, mechanical solidarity and Max Weber referred to it as social organization under traditional authority.

An example of small-group research which contributes to generic principles of order may be found in Jean Piaget's *The Moral Judgement of the Child* published in London in 1932. By playing marbles with groups of boys in Geneva, Switzerland he found that by age ten boys begin to socialize each other teaching each other that it is enforced rules which make the game possible and that enforced rules can bring freedom, in this case freedom from quarreling. They learn: no rules, no game, no game, no fun. Innovated rules which get repeated for some time become traditional. At the other end of the spectrum in his classic work on modern bureaucratized society Max Weber too stressed enforced rules as a source of freedom and order. He saw a bureaucratic rule of rules, rationally worked out, as maintaining order and efficiency by defining jurisdictions, and functions of office.

As a second main point of emphasis I believe that such a cross-cultural study, since our fast changing society is involved, would do well to make more use of a change-conscious frame of reference than is commonly done. We look out on the world of experience in two ways both of which are useful and necessary. We can use a static stance and regard change as the difference described when two or more assumed fixed points are compared. This makes possible measurement, taxonomy and logical analysis. We can also think of change as the differing itself which is process having the nature of a continuum. The former tends to direct attention to parts and classifications of parts, the latter to dynamic relations and systems. This will be treated more fully below.

## The Hutterite Population Now

The Hutterites have increased in number from the 3,721 in 33 colonies e-numerated by Dr. Eberhard Arnold in a colony-by-colony census in 1931 to an estimated over 20,000 in 200 colonies in 1972.[3] Computed on the basis of an annual rate of increase of well over four per cent which has been occurring in recent decades, their number in 1974 is probably between 21,500 and 22,000. Should the present rate of increase continue for another sixteen to seventeen years the population would double. Over three-fourths of the colonies are in Canada - in Alberta, Saskatchewan and Manitoba, in that order. Most colonies in the United States are in South Dakota and Montana. One has spilled over into Minnesota and one is located in Washington state west of Spokane. At least one colony is located in North Dakota.

Population increase has brought problems in its wake including litigative action aimed at control of their expansion. A comprehensive bibliography compiled by Marvin P. Riley includes thirty-eight annotated entries on legal aspects.[4] It is still more difficult to find satisfactory isolated sites for new colonies. For a while the Hutterites seriously considered moving to Paraguay but after sending two members there to investigate gave the idea up. Their population "explosion" in one way is probably helping them. Although much more prosperous now than during the Depression years, the need to buy more land for new colonies has served to prevent them from what they as diligent students of their history regard as one of their greatest perils, too much affluence.

## The Changing Hutterites

The Hutterites have modernized impressively the past few decades. Riley in a twenty-page introduction to his *Bibliography* and in a bulletin published in 1970 provides a recent description of change in the South Dakota communities.[5] In 1968 there were 2,772 Hutterites living in 27 colonies in

South Dakota. Average acreage, owned and rented, per colony had increased to 5,387 of which about three-fifths was in cropland, two-fifths in pasture. He reported that diversification of production was still very impressive and that self-sufficiency was still great though decreasing. All 27 colonies had a bulk milk operation and planted corn, 26 had a major beef enterprise and the same number grew sorghum, 25 each had large swine operations and large egg laying programs, 23 planted oats and the same number planted barley, and 23 kept bees. All 27 made the majority of their clothing, had gardens and did home canning, made their own laundry soap and repaired their shoes, while 20 had orchards and 13 made brooms. Use of modern farm machinery has increased. Riley reported that South Dakota Hutterites were using "track and diesel tractors to pull plows with as many as nine 14-inch bottoms or three subsoilers hitched in tandem." Poinsett colony founded in 1968 has a completely modern kitchen equipped with stainless steel and handy walk-in freezers. Its dining rooms have fluorescent lights and Formica-covered table tops. The apartments have running water and toilets. In all of the colonies the day when one slept floating between two feather ticks filled with goose down is gone; they now have mattresses. However some changes which have come to American rural life since 1939 have not reached the Hutterites. They have not become specialists in agri-business. They have not been suburbanized by the automobile. Although youth have illicit radios and television can be seen on occasion in town the electronic mass media is not making them over into we know not what. The Hutterites have their own kind of homogenization but now somewhat less of it. "Hutterites with more than grade school training are rare." Those who receive more instruction get it through correspondence courses. Up to 1970 the Hutterites in South Dakota were still succeeding in their resistance to integrated schools; Riley reported that "there is no colony in South Dakota where Hutterite children attend school with children from outside."

Some cracks in the Hutterite social structure have however occurred. The Saskatchewan Division of the Canadian Mental Health Association in Regina reported in 1953 that in the United States and Canada twenty-six Hutterite young men voluntarily enlisted in the armed forces during World War II. This would have been totally unthinkable in the nineteen thirties. It indicates a weakening which may be serious. Paul K. Conkin in 1964 stated that "several Hutterite colonies are helplessly unable to cope with deviant behavior and open irresponsibility among the youth."[6] He attributed the problem to situations where the isolation had greatly decreased and this sounds very convincing. Conkin found the total number of colonies in 1963 to be 142 with a population of about 14,000. In view of this number of colonies the undisclosed "several" would be a small per cent, not impressively larger than the number I encountered in the thirties. Conkin's excellent detailed description of Hutterite daily life and customs sounds almost identically the way I remember them in the thirties.

Like all predictions of the social future these days predictions of the future of the Hutterites is hazardous. When Eberhard Arnold returned to his home community, Rhonbruderhof in the Fulda district of Germany, after visiting all the Hutterite communities in 1930-31 he predicted disintegration of the

American Hutterite communities within the next twenty years "unless they are awakened to a new 'spirit' in lieu of their reliance on tradition."7 Thirty years later it was the Arnold movement which collapsed. I heard Arnold in 1931 reprove Hutterite leaders for remaining too strictly loyal to their traditions and for not going out into the world to do missionary work. Arnold had great charisma then, partly due to the contagious intensity of his faith and partly to the fact that as a student of church history he knew Hutterite history well. The Hutterites are worshipers of their history. Arnold received the degree of Doctor of Philosophy at the University of Erlangen in Bavaria. The title of his doctoral dissertation was "The Primitive Christian and Anti-Christian Elements in the Development of Friedrich Nietzsche." I of course disagree with Dr. Arnold on this point. In my opinion the future of the Hutterites depends upon ability to maintain sufficient isolation so loyalty to the traditions can be preserved. As for missionary work, the Hutterites gave up interest in that a few centuries ago. Anyone looking for a political Communist under the bed won't find a Hutterite. Conkin expressed the opinion that if and when disintegration sets in it will this time be terminal but adds that "future change will be slow and, at times, barely perceptible."8

*****

Max Weber in *The Protestant Ethic and the Spirit of Capitalism* provides an explanation for the Hutterite emphasis on community, beliefs and conscience. In writing about what he called "the Baptist movement and the sects" he was also writing about Anabaptist and thus Hutterite origins, though he made no reference to the Hutterites by name. The Hutterites emerged from the Anabaptist movement which originated near Zurich in 1523. Weber referred to these groups as "early Baptists", "Baptist sects" and "Swiss and South German Baptists." This can be confusing since the denomination now known as Baptists did not appear until some ninety years later. Perhaps Weber was reacting to an inconsistency inherent in the term, Anabaptist. It means to be baptized again which is a misnomer of a sort since Anabaptists denied the validity of the baptism administered to them when they were children.

Weber wrote: "we find a second independent source of Protestant asceticism besides Calvinism in the Baptist movement and the sects . . . whose ethics rest upon a basis differing in principle from the Calvinist doctrine."9 It might be called the second or other Protestant ethic. The Hutterites through their history have preserved it in close to pure type form.

Three key ideas in Weber's discussion concern community, beliefs, and conscience. Weber preferred to refer to these self-administered communities as sects rather than as churches for one could not be born into them and thus gain benefices and come under authority; one could only voluntarily join by an act of will when adult enough to have a faith of one's own based on beliefs. What one joined was a community and what the community had in common was not necessarily communal property; it was shared beliefs. Renunciation of the world was one of the beliefs. It was the Hutterites who took the extra step as an act of renunciation, namely the holding of property in common. To this day the Hutterites refer to beliefs where we would probably use the term, values.

Weber referred to these sects as communities of personal believers of the reborn. Equally important was conscience. Weber used concern about personal salvation as a constant. Only one who followed the dictates of conscience could be justified in considering himself as reborn.[10] Demonstration in the community life that one was following the dictates of conscience was regarded as an unchallengeable sign of true rebirth. Conscience was regarded as the means by which God communicates with man. One listens to an inner consciousness. However if one lives in community the chances are that community influences will do much to shape the conscience. This is certainly true in the Hutterite community. There conscience is a built-in control. The Anabaptist conscience was thus a socializing conscience supporting a social community ethic even though the concern was not so much about this world as the one after death.

Another source of social ethic was the fact that "life of the first generations of Christians was taken as a model. The Biblical way of life was conceived by the first Swiss and South German Baptists with a radicalism similar to that of the young St. Francis, as a sharp break with all the enjoyment of life, a life modeled directly on that of the Apostles."[11]

To borrow a term from Howard Becker, the culture case-history method would be of particular use in studying the Hutterites. They can be thought of as what they are in any now and also as what they have become through their history. Most of the significant becoming occurred during their formative first quarter-century when the system of beliefs was routinized and institutionalized. Considerably more research material on the history of the Hutterites is now available. Much of it is published in the *Mennonite Quarterly Review,* the *Mennonite Encyclopedia,* and *Mennonite Life.* A. J. F. Zieglschmid has made both Chronicles available in German with useful historic material appended.[12] Marvin P. Riley has compiled a valuable bibliography containing 322 annotated entries which is now being enlarged and revised.[13]

*****

Bergson has said that to undestand change "we must instal ourselves within it straight away."[14] William James who was influenced by Bergson has said much the same thing in a different way. "What really exists is not things made but things in the making . . . Put yourself in the making."[15] This applies to understanding life in a communal society such as the Hutterites partly because the communal experience is so different from our own but also because what is happening there is process. This of course is a matter of orientation, a way of looking out. In it, change, events and process provide what W.I. Thomas has called "the definition of the situation." Ralph Waldo Emerson put the orientation this way: "What is life but an endless flight of winged facts or events."[16] John Dewey has said "the matter of science is a character of events and changes as they change."[17] Leibnitz must have been reaching for this dynamic definition of the situation when he said, "What does not act does not exist; only what is actual is real."

However, the dynamic kind of orientation possessed by Heraclitus, Vico, Emerson, Bergson, James, Dewey, Whitehead and McIver, among others, does not come "straight away" and Bergson would be the last to say that it does. In fact he has said that putting oneself inside a continuous process of change, experiencing it from the inside, is a difficult thing for our Occidental culture has habituated us to think in terms of solids which can be cut up into bits or represented by points on a line. When we recompose such fragments, perhaps using logic, we tell ourselves that we have arrived at understanding. What is missing is (1) the relations between things which is at least as important as the things, and (2) how the interrelating and interacting occurs. The language one uses in thinking contributes to the difficulty. A great many of the terms and concepts one uses when doing the inner talking to oneself we call thinking, express the idea of fixed states more than motion. Reared in Occidental culture one tends to be a hard headed, hard nosed, solid, substantial thinker. Hardness seems to have a special value. H. Wittgenstein has said: "If we spoke a different language we would perceive a somewhat different world." Overorientation in stasis becomes a problem when survival depends upon adaptation to accelerating change for how we look out on change affects ability to direct it as we can and to adapt to it as we must. Some reorientation is needed.

How acquire such a reorientation? Probably soaking oneself in ecological thinking which seems to be as much philosophy as science, would help. The ecologist looks for moving forms of interrelating, interdepending and inter-acting, in an environment. Small wonder that Shepherd and McKay call ecology the subversive science.[19] It demands a dynamic, non-static way of looking out. Once inoculated with the ecological point of view nothing can be quite the same again. One thinks in a different language. On this point Lewis Mumford has said, "All thinking worthy of the name must now be ecological."[20]

Another method of achieving the reorientation would be to go back to Heraclitus and move up through history spending much time with Giambattista Vico. To James Joyce the Heraclitan path, via Lucretius, became in *Finnegan's Wake,* "the Vico road" which goes round and round to meet where terms began. Vico's *Autobiography* (1731) is at least as stimulating as his *The New Science,* which reached its second edition in 1730.[21] Vico's published dynamite, *La Scienza Nuova* carried an endorsement by no less than Cardinal Corsini who became Pope Clement XII to whom the second editions was dedicated.

A history of Western thought about change would be useful since it would show us how we came to think as we do. About 500 B.C. the Greeks came to a fork in the road, one personified in Heraclitus, prophet of process, the other in Pythagorus who literally worshipped numbers in a mystical way. Pythagorus won and we lost. We have the Fragments of Heraclitus because they were quoted and requoted in effort to refute him.[22] Dewey has offered an explanation for the resistance to Heraclitus. "In the classic philosophy, the ideal world is essentially a haven in which men find rest from the storms of life; it is an asylum in which he takes refuge from the troubles of existence with the calm assurance that it alone is supremely real."[23]

Plato and Aristotle quoted Heraclitus as saying in effect, "all things flow, nothing abides." In the flow Heraclitus saw forms and the forms frequently had the nature of juxtapositions of opposites or assumed opposites. For him wholes so formed were sources of insight. He spoke of this as "hidden harmony." Harmonization and reconciliation of opposites was for him a goal. "In change one finds rest." "Were there no injustice men would never know the name of justice." "It is disease that makes health pleasant; evil, good; hunger, plenty; weariness, rest." "Out of discord comes the fairest harmony." He spoke like an astronaut or Buckminster Fuller, and certainly like a relativist, when he said, "The way up and the way down is one and the same." When the Heraclitan reference frame is used change and causation become different approaches to the same thing. Whoever compares Hutterite order with our order, including lack of it, will find himself working with a Heraclitan kind of whole, order-disorder, or if you will, order-anomie.

As the Hutterites have come down through their history meeting the challenge of change a set of central or basic values integrated into a system has served them. Being a community of religious believers who place much emphasis on belief, they prefer the term, *Die Glauben,* the beliefs. Probably the most unifying value is the belief that collective interests must take priority over individual interests when the two clash. The value system serves like a Constitution with reference to which the new and untried is tested for consistency. Decision is by consensus guided by community-trained conscience attuned to beliefs and traditions. Thus, to borrow a term from Sumner, the system has a built-in "strain toward consistency" in the form of an ethos with an integrated value center. In 1919 Yeats cried out from colonial Ireland, "things fall apart, the center cannot hold." But where and what is our value center?

Lee Emerson Deets<br>
October 1974

[1] Harris, Louis, *The Agony of Change,* W.W. Norton Co., 1973, p.277.

[2] Toennies, Ferdinand, *Gemeinschaft und Gesellschaft,* 1887, published in English in 1940 as *Fundamental Concepts of Sociology: Gemeinschaft und Gesellschaft,* Charles P. Loomis, translator.

[3] Associated Press dispatch from Tabor, South Dakota, January 9, 1972 citing a Hutterite estimate.

[4] Riley, Marvin P., *The Hutterite Brethren, An Annotated Bibliography with Special Reference to South Dakota Hutterite Colonies,* Agricultural Experiment Station Bulletin 529, South Dakota State University, Brookings, 1965.

5 Riley, Marvin P., *South Dakota's Hutterite Colonies, 1874-1969,* Agricultural Experiment Station Bulletin 565, South Dakota State University, Brookings, 1970.

6 Conkin, Paul K., *Two Paths to Utopia, The Hutterites and the Llano Colony,* University of Nebraska Press, Lincoln, 1964, p. 190.

7 Benepe, Jagna Wojcicki, *An Analysis of the Growth and Stability of the Bruderhof Movement,* Unpublished M.A. thesis, Hunter College, 1957, p. 17, citing Minutes of Woodcrest Household Meeting, August 3, 1956. This was a study of Woodcrest Bruderhof in Ulster county New York, one of the communal communities in the movement founded under the leadership of Eberhard Arnold in 1920 which affiliated with the American Hutterites in 1931. The Minutes cited were in possession of Woodcrest Bruderhof.

8*Ibid.,* pp.99-100

9 Weber, Max, *The Protestant Ethic and the Spirit of Capitalism,* George Allen & Unwin, Ltd., London, 1930, Translated by Talcott Parsons, p. 144, and "The Baptist Sects," 144-154. See also *From Max Weber,* translated and edited by H.H. Gerth and C. Wright Mills, Oxford Univ. Press, 1946, Ch. XII "The Protestant Sects and the Spirit of Capitalism."

10Weber, *The Protestant Ethic,* p. 148

11Weber, *The Protestant Ethic,* p. 146

12Zieglschmid, A.J.F. (ed.), *Das Klein Geschichtbuch der Huttischen Brüder,* The Carl Schurz Memorial Foundation, Inc. Philadelphia, 1947; *Die Alteste Chronik der Hutterischen Brüder,* The Carl Schurz Memorial Foundation, Inc. 1943.

13Riley, op. cit.

14 Bergson, Henri, *Creative Evolution,* Random House, pp. 324-5.

15 James, William, *A Pluralistic Universe,* Longmans Green, 1928, p. 263.

16Emerson, R.W., "History", *Essays by Ralph Waldo Emerson,* Apollo edition, Crowell, 1961, p. 24.

17 Dewey, John, *Experience and Nature,* Open Court Publishing Co., Macmillan, 1929, Chap. X "Process".

19 Shepherd, Paul, and Daniel McKay, editors, *The Subversive Science, Essays Toward an Ecology of Man,* Houghton, 1969.

20 Chisholm, Anne, *Philosophers of the Earth, Conversations with Ecologists,* E.P. Dutton & Co., p. 15.

21 Fisch, M.H., and T.G. Bergin, *Vico, His Autobiography,* Cornell University Press, 1944. The authors have also translated his *La Scienza Nuova.*

22 Bakewell, Charles M., *Source Book in Ancient Philosophy,* Charles Scribner's Sons, 1939, chap. III, "Heraclitus", based on Diels translation of *Heraklit* from Greek and German.

23 Dewey, John, *Reconstruction in Philosophy,* Mentor Book, New American Library, 1950, (paper), p. 103.

# APPENDIX

Reprinted for private circulation from
PUBLICATION OF THE SOCIOLOGICAL SOCIETY OF AMERICA
Vol. XXV, No. 2, May, 1931
PRINTED IN THE U.S.A.

# THE ORIGINS OF CONFLICT IN THE HUTTERISCHE COMMUNITIES

LEE EMERSON DEETS
University of South Dakota

### ABSTRACT

The Hutterische Brüder are a sectarian communistic society comprising thirty-two colonies, four in South Dakota and twenty-eight in Manitoba and Alberta, which trace their origin in 1528 to the Anabaptist movement in Moravia. Their history and culture formation is a record of crisis, persecution, and frequent migration into isolation. The community life is greatly restricted in contact and is on a simple culture level. It is controlled by a religious oligarchy at times verging on autocracy. It is a primary group par excellence but without the control of gossip. Adult quarrelling is almost unknown in recent years. The individual is submerged in the community. The extreme solidarity of the community, together with its isolation, provides a good set-up for the study of community conflict origins. Conflicts in the Hutterische communities may be divided into two major types, outside and internal. They are caused by the enmity of the family and the community, the desire for money operating as a beginning point for the introduction of individualism into communism, and lastly, the breakdown of isolation.

Although little heard of, the first communistic community to be founded is still in existence with solidarity unimpaired.[1] It is the longest lived and the strongest of the several hundred experimental community utopias which have come and mostly gone. As a society made up of a number of communities, it has passed the last half-century of its over four centuries of existence in the James and Missouri River valleys of South Dakota. Its extreme degree of mutual aid and isolation make it a unique and laboratory-like set-up for the study of community. This analysis of the more important internal conflicts in the Hutterische communities is a part of a larger study now being made of factors in their common life.

The Hutterische Brüder, Hutterians, or Hutterites, all of which they are commonly called, originated as a sectarian communistic society in Moravia (now modern Czechoslovakia) in the year 1528 as a part of the Anabaptist movement, which itself was a product of the Protestant reformation. Their practice of community of goods, always incidental to their religion, began as an emergency measure in the pooling of their possessions while in flight from Nicolsburg

[1] Preliterate communal organization, ancient village communities, the Russian mir, Chinese familism, and monasticism originated, of course, before 1528, but are of a different type.

in 1528, and has as a religious basis Acts 2:44, 45.[2] Created in crisis and developed in unprecedented martyrdom,[3] a culture arose which with few lapses has been largely adhered to for over four centuries. The colonies today present the striking phenomenon of sixteenth-century crisis and culture projected into twentieth-century American life. They have passed through two periods totaling approximately 115 years when individual was substituted for common ownership of property.[4]

The four centuries of history of the existing Hutterische communities may be divided into five periods. They are now entering a sixth. A little less than a century (1528–1622)[5] was spent in Moravia, approximately a century and a half (1622–1770) in Transylvania and Wallachia (now Rumania),[6] a little over a century in Russia (1770–1873), over a half-century since 1874–77 in South Dakota, and since 1917 the movement has been to Manitoba and Alberta, Canada. Hutterian history has fortunately been preserved in their own chronicles, written in longhand and discovered only recently by historians. The *Grossgeschichtbuch,* recording early history, went to press in Vienna in 1923, edited by Rudolph Wolkan, under the title, *Geschicht-Buch der Hutterischen Brüder.* The *Kleingeschichtbuch,* covering later centuries, is now in press in the same city.

In viewing their history, dramatic though their chronicles are as the record of a unique type of group conflict, space permits here only the briefest résumé of one aspect, their persecution, which is essential for interpretation of the present community solidarity and conflict. The first intense period of persecution began in 1535, resulting a year later in the martyrdom of their leader, Jacob Huter. This had hardly subsided when a second period of persecution began in 1548, to be followed (1565–92) by the "ideal period for the

[2] "And all that believed were together, and had all things common; and sold their possessions and goods, and parted them to all men, as every man had need."

[3] John Horsch, "The Hutterian Brethren, 1528–1929. A Story of Martyrdom and Loyalty," *Mennonite Quarterly Review* (April, 1929), II, 97–102; Johann Loserth, "The Decline and Revival of the Hutterites," *ibid.* (April, 1930), IV, 93.

[4] 1686–1761 and 1819–59.

[5] Except 1548–52 when banished for a short period to Hungary.

[6] Some went to Hungary, later to be converted to Catholicism or driven out.

church" during which their numbers increased from the original two or three hundred to between twelve and fifteen thousand living in from forty to fifty Brüderhöfe or communal communities. In 1605 an invasion of the Turks, Tartars, and Hungarians caused the destruction of sixteen Brüderhöfe in three months, the death of 81 members, the enslavement of 250 others, and the confiscation of much property. In 1619 an army of King Ferdinand of Austria invaded Moravia, destroying twelve and devastating seventeen more of the colonies, resulting in death, destruction, violation, and enslavement of women and children. By 1621 one-third of the membership was lost by death through sword and plague, and the number of colonies was reduced to twenty-four. Five years later less than a thousand members were left. Subsequent events include another Turkish invasion (1664–65), persistent attempts to force baptism of children (1725), an attack by the Jesuits (1759–60), and expulsion by the Empress Maria Theresa, including an attempt to put their children in orphanages. The *Geschicht-Buch* records an enormous number of martyrs, giving their names and places of execution.

From Russia the Hutterites came to Dakota territory in 1874–76, and established three Brüderhöfe in what is now southeastern South Dakota. By 1918 these three had increased by a process of colonization to seventeen. In 1917, because of distrust of their German culture (although they had been separated from Germany for many centuries), their conscientious objection to war, and their restricted participation in outside affairs, external conflict arose which started the Hutterites on their latest trek in search of a location for their utopia, this time in Canada. In 1922 the Hutterites numbered 2,622 living in twenty-six colonies. At the present time they live in thirty-two colonies—three in South Dakota, twenty-nine in Canada—and are estimated to number well over 3,000. Of the three remaining in South Dakota two plan to move when they can sell their land, and the third, Bon Homme colony located on the Missouri River between Yankton and Springfield, has no present plans for moving.

An interesting aspect of the Hutterian colonization process is the beginning of what in the future very probably may be three sects within the sect. The cleavage is being formed not on the basis of conscious conflict but through the relation of the offspring colonies to the three original South Dakota colonies, as shown in the accompanying diagram.

THE THREE CLEAVAGES OF HUTTERISCHE COMMUNITIES*

I. The "Schmiede Leut' "

| Bon Homme | Milltown | James Valley |
| | | Blumen Gard |
| | | Rosedale    Iberville |
| | Huron | Ihorndale |
| | Maxwille | Barrickman |
| | (or Maxwell) | |
| | Bon Homme (Can.) | |

II. The "Darius Leut' "

| Wolf Creek | Jamesville | Ost-Cardston |
| | | Richards |
| | | Spring Valley |
| | Lake Byron | |
| | West-Raley | Pincher |
| | Rosebud | Bysieker |
| | Stand Off | Grenum |

III. The "Lehrer Leut' "

| Old Elm Spring | Rockport | Rockport (Can.) |
| | New Elm Spring | Milford    Miama |
| | | Big Bend |
| | | An un-named colony |
| | Old Elm Spring (Can.) | |

* The underlined colonies are in South Dakota (1931). All others have gone to or were colonized in Canada since 1917.

The "Lehrer Leut'," which takes its name from the school teacher leader of Old Elm Spring community, is the most liberal. Its members wear buttons instead of hooks and eyes, associate more easily with outside people, and look more favorably upon community use of automobiles. The most conservative group, the "Schmiede Leut' " colonies and their colonized offspring, branched off from Bon Homme colony which was led from Russia by a blacksmith. The "Darius Leut' " take their name from the leader, Darius Walter, who brought Wolf Creek colony from Russia. Unification within each of the three groups is developing along economic, social, and religious lines, although checked temporarily by the movement to Canada. Corporation charters, which were removed by Supreme Court decision in South Dakota, have been renewed in Canada. Business records for the three groups are kept separate. Gifts and business transactions such as loans occur between colonies of the separate groups, but seldom between colonies outside their own group. Social correspondence and visiting, largely because of closer kinship, occurs more between colonies within the separate groups than without. Policies are determined largely within the three groups, although an attempt is made once a year to have a representative meeting of all colonies. There is a tripartite "we group" consciousness developing within the larger distinct Hutterian "consciousness of kind," and the process is in the making.

As a background let us turn to a brief picture of a Hutterische colony. One comes upon a Hutterische colony at the end of some forgotten road, or a winding road in a well-wooded river valley makes a sudden turn and the panorama of stone buildings, apparently innumerable geese, quaintly garbed people, and Oberammergau-like bearded faces makes him wonder if he has been magically transported into Central Europe of reformation times. Closer observation, revealing tractors, grain elevators, and other modern machinery out of place in the picture, soon dispels such an illusion. For, dwelling in this old-world seclusion, are up-to-date farmers who read the trade journals, utilize the laboratories of their state university, and consult the expert advice of their state college of agriculture. Closer inspection reveals the minute order which governs the place.[7] There are the two-story, stone, kitchenless apartment houses, uniformly furnished, each providing living quarters for a dozen or two families. One sees the spacious common dining-hall with a kitchen at one end, the building serving as church and school, the large massive barns of stone and wood, the bakery, old grist mill, laundry, broom shop, tannery, carpenter shop, smith shop, apiary, and kindergarten. This latter institution, created cen-

---

[7] From this point on, the description and analysis is largely based on Bon Homme colony.

turies before the modern kindergarten, each day assumes responsibility over children who are two and a half to six years old. As one goes about, the plan of the place unfolds. It is a community, an area of nearly adequate service, within a neighborhood. The spirit of the place is co-operation and organization. Each woman knows that out of each twelve weeks she will spend one week in the kitchen and one week in the bakery, and that out of each three weeks she will spend a week milking cows and a week washing dishes. Among the many occupations held by men there is a cattle boss, a sheep boss, a hog boss, and over all agriculture a farm boss. Supreme over all things temporal is "the Boss," and over things spiritual is the minister. These are counseled and checked by a group of five to seven elders known as "headquarters." If in the rise of natural leadership the minister or the "boss" comes to assume control, the oligarchy of elders tends to verge upon an autocracy of natural leadership. The sovereignty of the leader seems to rest in the sense of security the members of his colony have as a result of the decisions he makes for them. The other social controls of the community are unique adaptations to the needs and conditions peculiar to the community. Although a primary group par excellence, gossip does not exist as a form of social control. "What right has one child of God to talk about another?" they question. The nature of the social controls responsible for the exceptional, in fact historically unprecedented, solidarity of this community is much too great a subject for inclusion in this paper.

Most unique in the community is its lack of conflict. This very lack creates a significant field for the study of conflict in its origins and less complex forms. Adult quarreling in the community is practically unheard of in recent years. The individual tends to become submerged in the community. Modern individualism, like tobacco, arose since the community culture patterns were cast and is taboo. This solidarity is particularly striking when one realizes that several hundred communistic communities have come and for the most part have passed out of existence since the Hutterische origins in 1528. What are conflicts which ordinarily destroy this type of community life, and which the Hutterites have thus far been unable to survive? A few comparisons throw some light. The Shakers disagreed among themselves over retention of outworn folkways and mores and were slowly and steadily destroyed by their celibacy. The Hutterische, by enforced migration into isolation, have had their mores protected from change too rapid for readjustment and reintegration. They have had no sex taboos necessitating celibacy, and through colonization have solved the problem of increased population without resorting to celibacy. Leadership has been another important factor in conflict and solidarity in community life. The Doukhobors[8] faced near disaster when leaderless in a period of migration to and very difficult adjustment in a new country. Oneida community suffered from a change in type if not in quality of leadership and from a decline in the original drive which created the community. A prominent citizen of the Amana Society gave the writer as major factors making for disorganization in that community, "the lessening influence of the founders on each succeeding generation—I would place that first—and second in importance, a constantly increasing influence of outside ideas." Zoar's beginning of decline dates from the death of their founder-leader, after which problems of declining prosperity and of increasing outside contacts, individualism, and insubordination became greater than could be met.[9] With the Hutterites, severe persecution held them together during the period of their early history, until the time when their mores had been so strengthened and crystallized that the sanctity of custom supplied the momentum to carry them through times of weak leadership. The Hutterische communities, up to the present time, have survived, but have within their community life the germs of future conflict. The account of their external conflict with county, state, and nation cannot be given here. It is primarily an analysis of culture conflict, and has in it the drama of life and death in war-camp prisons and of a losing battle in the Supreme Court for the right to retain their charter as a corporation.

Foremost among the internal conflicts in the Hutterische community is the natural enmity existing there between the institutions, family and community. We witness in the Hutterische community

---

[8] Maude Aylmer, *A Peculiar People, the Doukhobors,* p. 173 (New York: Funk & Wagnalls).

[9] E. O. Randall, *History of Zoar Society,* pp. 47-54.

a sociological battle between two basic institutions, with the community at least at present holding the upper hand. The community is an enemy of the family because first of all it defunctionalizes the family. In this it resembles the effects of modern urbanization upon family life outside. In the Hutterische community the economic unity of the family is practically nil. The father of a Hutterische family has no more economic responsibility for his own family than for any other family in the community. The mother has no economic function in preparing the food for her own family. These functions pass to the community kitchen and dining-hall. Children are not habituated to look to the family for support, and do not learn the home economics of household management. The one or two rooms in which a family ordinarily lives and sleeps are hardly adequate for development of home loyalty and family "we group" consciousness. The head of the family is not directly master of his domicile, for such policies as whether he shall have more room for an enlarging family or less room for a decreasing one, are determined by the elders. The community also takes over almost completely the educational function of the family. At the age of two and a half the child passes out of the care of the mother for most of the day, including meal hours. A great part of the problem of disciplining children and youth is left to one appointed for that purpose. The "boss" of the colony tends to absorb in a patriarchal way the authority of the father. The common reply in Bon Homme colony is, "Ask Mike," referring of course to the minister-"boss." The community also absorbs social functions of the family. Family privacy is little known, for community members are constantly entering and leaving without knocking. Work and social contacts within the community are almost always on the larger group basis, although visiting follows kinship lines.

But the family is also the enemy of the community. When an issue arises, loyalty to the family is very likely to be greater than loyalty to the community. The Hutterische community, in spite of centuries of culture control, cannot prevent the innate drive of parental love from putting family loyalties first. Because the community taboos dolls and allows insufficient money for candy and simple toys, rifts of deep-seated origin lie simmering underneath. The conflict, although of paramount potential significance, is only latent. The community partially meets it by becoming more liberal in distributing candy as a community function.

The family, in the Hutterische community, becomes the point of invasion of capitalism into communism.[10] It has long been recognized that the family tends to demand recognition of private property.[11] Oneida community in abolishing the conventional family, was, from the standpoint of preserving communistic community solidarity, theoretically right, although this was not its major purpose in so doing. In the past, both celibacy and communism of wives, as well as the "complex marriage" of Oneida community, have operated to check the challenge of the family to the community.[12] Dowie, founder of Zion City, required his followers to sign a vow "that all family ties and obligations . . . . be held subordinate."[13] The fact remains that all men and all families are not equal and that differences in ability, temperament, and needs arise to demand recognition. Systems of nearly complete communism of goods, such as the Hutterische communities, have been able to keep these differences from developing beyond a minimum. Systems of partial communism of good, such as the Amana Society, by leaving room for greater recognition of differences in economic status, result in greater individualism.

The desire for money and its purchasing power, already referred to in connection with the Hutterische family, is of even wider significance as a potential cause of conflict. Contrary to conditions in the world outside, security is not a factor in it, but in actuality serves as a check upon it, since anything which threatens the solidarity of the community, threatens the security of the individual member. Among the children money is simply a symbol of candy credit. Among adults, in addition to functions already referred to, it is a symbol of increased freedom to secure more of the expanding life revealed by increased contacts with outside society. That the danger of the desire for money to the community solidarity is fully

[10] The Hutterische communities in their relationships with the outside world are distinctly capitalistic.

[11] Karl Kautsky, *Communism in Central Europe*, pp. 16–17.

[12] *Ibid.*        [13] Quoted by Mark Sullivan in *Our Times*, III, 497–98.

realized by Hutterische community leaders is attested to by this statement made by one of them: "It happens to the younger boys. They wish money. But we watch that. Kill it out as soon as it happens. Don't allow them to do it. Money and idle time are bad."

Other conflicts arising are: (1) a recognized discrepancy between the outworn folkways or mores and present conditions. The use of automobiles and the permitting of one's photograph to be taken are taboos which are becoming seriously questioned. Folkways and mores are cast off by an interesting process of rationalization. (2) Social control conflicts over work assignments, strictness of management, punishment for infraction of rules, and distribution of privileges such as making trips to nearby towns. (3) Conflicts caused by increasing contacts with outside culture, initiating the beginnings or nuclei of nebulous conflict groups around new behavior patterns.

Germs of internal conflict in the Hutterische communities may, in conclusion, be briefly summarized as follows:

1. Defunctionalization of the family by the community.
2. Usurping of loyalty from the community by the family.
3. Desire for money to spend on one's own children.
4. Desire for money to purchase marginal goods not supplied.
5. Permission to make trips out of the community.
6. Irksome survival of out-lived folkways and mores.
7. Unpleasant work assignments.
8. Strictness of management.
9. Disapproval over administration policies.
10. Question of the supremacy of leadership between the "boss" and the minister.
11. Punishment and discipline.
12. Policies regarding purchase of land.
13. Policies regarding liberalization—product of culture conflict.
14. Introduction of new culture patterns—product of culture conflict.
15. Influences arising from employment of outside teacher and labor.
16. Conflicts of children at play.
17. Jealousy, potential but now individually controlled.
18. Mental conflicts and desires unsatisfied by the community.
    a) Postponement of marriage, and non-marriage.
    b) Desires for cars, travel, and light-colored dresses "with flowers."
19. Realization by some parents of the lack of opportunity for superior children.
20. Emergence of sect-like groupings produced by colonization.

Lastly, it should be pointed out that in spite of the long history and present solidarity of this community, the principles of communistic living exemplified in it are hardly applicable to the great society. Values to be sought in such a study lie more largely in the contribution to theories of community association. Communal living, to be successful, requires great sacrifice. Such a sacrificial spirit can exist only when motivated by a powerful drive. In the history of communistic communities thus far, only religion has furnished such a drive. The world at large is not religious enough to be sacrificial enough to make the Hutterian type of communism successful.

# NOTES

# NOTES

# NOTES